Advanc

"Bianca D'Alessio's *Mastering Intentions* is a transformative journey into the art of intentional living. Through her powerful storytelling and practical wisdom, Bianca inspires us to embrace authenticity, vulnerability, and purpose as the foundation for a truly fulfilling life. This book is a must-read for anyone ready to align their energy, focus, and actions with their highest potential."

—**Marie Diamond**, Global Transformational Teacher and Feng Shui Master

"Bianca is a powerful force and radiant light. *Mastering Intentions* is a physical manifest of Bianca's core being, soul, and mind. It's a guide to becoming. This book reveals a glimpse of her internal thought process, crazy beautiful mind, and inspires us to discover our power from within to unlock our highest self."

—**Christina Carmona**, Founder of Island to East Side

"Bianca stands in her truth, does the deep work, and generously shares her wisdom in *Mastering Intentions*. This book is for women who are ready to step into their power and lead with authenticity. Bianca's ten practices are not just words on a page—they're a reflection of her lived experience, offering the kind of insight that only comes from someone who has done the work herself."

—**Tory Archbold**, CEO Powerful Steps

"Bianca the epitome of living, leading, and succeeding authentically. In a world where perfection is prized, her message is a breath of fresh air. *Mastering Intentions* is a powerful guide to breaking free from societal expectations, embracing your true self, and unleashing the transformative power of intention. A must-read for anyone wanting to deliver authentic and lasting impact."

—**Alison Shamir**, Impostor Syndrome Expert, International Speaker, and Author

"Bianca's book is a powerful reminder that life doesn't have to be about the 'or'—we can embrace the 'and.'"

—**Hilary DeCesare**, Celebrity Success Coach, Master Nuero-Performance Coach, The ReLaunch

"Bianca's journey is a testament to the transformative power of intention. I have had the pleasure of seeing it form into an incredible brand and leadership that carry forward one of the most successful teams in the world and in a very competitive industry. *Mastering Intentions* is based on real experience and provides a clear path to personal and professional growth through vulnerability, purpose, and authenticity."

—**Eddie Shapiro**, President CEO Nest Seekers International

"Every generation has a book that becomes their blueprint for success. Bianca D'Alessio has created it for GenZ and everyone before and after. If you want the recipe for identifying and achieving your purpose, then *Mastering Intentions* is your bible. Brava, Bianca!"

—**Dr. Tara Chalakani**, Mental Health Expert, Co-host of *Welloff Podcast*

"Far more than a guide, Bianca's book is the Good to Great for that dynamic relationship between personal and professional growth as well as the overall arc of leadership in the workplace. It is a staple on my shelf of best business books."

—**Cliff Oxford**, Founder, CliffCo, STI Knowledge, Oxford Center for Entrepreneurs

MASTERING INTENTIONS

10 PRACTICES TO AMPLIFY YOUR POWER AND LEAD WITH LASTING IMPACT

BIANCA D'ALESSIO

SAVIO
REPVBLIC

A SAVIO REPUBLIC BOOK
An Imprint of Post Hill Press
ISBN: 979-8-88845-864-8
ISBN (eBook): 979-8-88845-865-5

Mastering Intentions:
10 Practices to Amplify Your Power and Lead with Lasting Impact
© 2025 by Bianca D'Alessio
All Rights Reserved

Cover Photo by Frank Nannariello, Lucid Horizon

This book, as well as any other Savio Republic publications, may be purchased in bulk quantities at a special discounted rate. Contact orders@posthillpress.com for more information.

All people, locations, events, and situations are portrayed to the best of the author's memory. While all of the events described are true, many names and identifying details have been changed to protect the privacy of the people involved.

No part of this book may be reproduced, stored in a retrieval system, or transmitted by any means without the written permission of the author and publisher.

SAVIO
REPVBLIC

posthillpress.com
New York • Nashville
Published in the United States of America

1 2 3 4 5 6 7 8 9 10

Table of Contents

Introduction: Foundation to *Mastering Intentions* vii

INTENTION ONE: ACTIVATE YOUR PERSONAL PURPOSE

- Practice 1: Articulate Your Personal Purpose 3
- Practice 2: Activate with Intention 27
- Practice 3: Act Purposefully 50

INTENTION TWO: AMPLIFY YOUR POWER

- Practice 4: Harness Your Inner Confidence 79
- Practice 5: Adopt a Winner's Mindset 108
- Practice 6: Manifest Your Future 144
- Practice 7: Create Empowering Habits 178

INTENTION THREE: LEAD WITH LASTING IMPACT

- Practice 8: Foster Teamship 215
- Practice 9: Lead with Authenticity 235
- Practice 10: Unlock the Power of Gratitude 256

What's Next? Let's Be Intentional Together 273
Acknowledgments 281
About the Author 285

To each and every one of my companions who have walked beside me on life's journey—through triumphs and trials, through clarity and chaos—your presence has been both my anchor and my fuel. You have shaped my path, reminding me that intention is not just about the goals we set, but about the people who uplift and support us along the way.

To Professor Mulcahy, whose wisdom and belief in me illuminated paths I had yet to see—your guidance has been a quiet force, strengthening my resolve and sharpening my vision.

With gratitude beyond words, I thank you all.

Introduction

Foundation to Mastering Intentions

I remember stepping on set to film the first season of *Selling the Hamptons*[1] on MAX. Hiding behind my big smile and loud, nervous laugh were my sweaty hands and a head filled with anxious thoughts as I wondered, "What do I do now?"

My producer turned to me and said, "Now is your time. You can tell your story your way, or you can allow the outside world to write their own narrative. The power is yours."

While it wasn't in that exact moment, in the following months of filming I finally found power in vulnerability and storytelling by writing my own narrative and embracing my story. By owning my story and leaning into the lessons of the hardships, I was able to see that these experiences served as stepping stones and were, in fact, the driving forces that have shaped

---

[1] *Selling the Hamptons*, produced by Nick Rigg, Eddie Shapiro and Tony DiSanto, featuring Bianca D'Alessio, Mia Calabrese, Michael Fulfree, Peggy Zabakolas, and J.B. Andreassi, premiered on January 20, 2022, on MAX, https://www.max.com/shows/selling-the-hamptons/b425b881-93a3-49be-a896-dd8100edf12a.

me into the woman I have grown into today. This explorative journey has allowed me to propel my business, enhance my relationships, and unlock the mental constructs that were holding me back from ultimate liberation—emotionally, physically, financially, and professionally.

Prior to this realization I had somewhat of a fixation with perfection—always trying to put myself into the box I felt society wanted me to fit into. "Don't be emotional," because society respects stoicism and strength, but don't become "too strong" because then you will never be in a relationship. "Don't have kids," because then you will compromise your career, but be prepared for the line of questioning and cross-eyed looks. Own your voice, but "don't be too loud." Be compassionate, but not "too compassionate," so that you don't get taken advantage of.

I became so fixated on what society said I should be that I started losing track of who I actually was. I began questioning—how can I create an intentional life if I wasn't being honest with myself? In time, I realized I can be both independently confident but also in a committed relationship, lead with a philanthropic heart but also be a no-nonsense businesswoman, have a successful career while also being the keystone to my family.

I could be strong, but also vulnerable. Life didn't need to be about the "or"—I could be "both"; I could be "and." I could be whatever I wanted to be—I could build whatever life I wanted to live—I just needed to rediscover myself and build a life filled with intention.

The quality of your life is shaped by the intentions that you set. Every action you take, every decision you make, and every dream you pursue is born from a core intention. But what if you could master this force—intention itself—to transform your life into one of purpose, fulfillment, and genuine success?

Mastering Intentions is a call to action to live a life of clarity, purpose, and fulfillment. My intention is to help you achieve your goals, align them with your core values, and unlock your full potential.

Imagine waking up every day with a sense of clarity and direction, knowing that your actions are aligned with your deepest values. *Mastering Intentions* provides proven tools to define your purpose and live more intentionally, not just reacting to life as it happens. Exercises in this book will help you discover and articulate your personal purpose. I'll guide you through proven self-reflection and visualization exercises around articulating the values, aspirations, and the driving forces behind the life you want to lead. The practices in this book will empower your decisions with action. You will learn to activate your personal purpose, amplify your personal power, and practice more intentional leadership for lasting impact.

It's not enough to know your values; *Mastering Intentions* shows you how to purposefully activate them daily. Whether evaluating your relationships through a Companion Audit, setting meaningful goals, or making empowered decisions, you'll learn practices to translate your purpose into concrete, intentional actions from a place of greater inner alignment. My personal purpose is to lead with vulnerability and authenticity, allowing me to build a business that prioritizes the growth and self-development of people. *Mastering Intentions* is all about understanding and aligning with personal purpose. It is through living intentionally that I find incredible energy in helping others on their journey of personal growth and excellence.

Once you activate your intentions, the next outcome you can expect is to amplify your personal power. It is more than feeling confident: it's about harnessing your inner energy for tangible results. Cultivating a winner's mindset, practicing positive self-talk, and future casting your aspirations are all essential tools to do so. By completing these exercises, you'll build greater self-efficacy, amplifying your power to navigate inevitable life challenges and manifest the future you envision for yourself.

Mastering Intentions doesn't just focus on your individual success. This book is also about leading with lasting impact, both in your personal life and in your career. You'll learn how to cultivate meaningful, intentional relationships that reflect your values, and you'll master new tools to lead with authenticity and collaboration. Whether you're leading a team at work or fostering deeper connections with loved ones, this section on how to lead with lasting impact will help create environments of growth, gratitude, and collective empowerment.

What Sets *Mastering Intentions* Apart?

Mastering Intentions differs from other self-development books out there in three key ways:

1) **Grounded in Purpose, Not Just Habits.** I have personally benefited from many of the practices described in books that focus on changing habits or improving performance, particularly those from *Atomic Habits* by James Clear[2]. I wrote *Mastering Intentions* to go one step further and ground actions to personal purpose: *I help you explore why you do what you do before focusing on the how.* I show you how to push beyond practicing better habits to more *intentionally* align those habits with who you truly are and what you deeply care about. It's about

---

[2] James Clear, *Atomic Habits* (New York City: Avery Publishing, 2018).

emotional transformation—rediscovering yourself, embracing vulnerability, and leading authentically. This book encourages you to reflect on your life experiences, acknowledge your challenges, and use them as stepping stones to become the person you are meant to be. It's a journey of self-awareness, resilience, and emotional liberation, all designed to help you build a life of fulfillment.

2) **Integrates "Innerwork" with "Teamship."** The books I have read offer many powerful individual strategies for self-growth. We cannot operate and grow in isolation: our work and our personal lives are increasingly interdependent with others! *Mastering Intentions* adds something that is less talked about and more critical to our performance in the next decade: the integration of Innerwork and Teamship. We have to go beyond learning how to improve ourselves. We must learn to foster deeper connections with others and build collaborative, empowering environments. Focusing on personal growth and collective success, I provide a more relevant and holistic approach to tapping into the power of shared intentions and teamwork.

3) **Focuses on Long-Lasting Impact.** The principles in this book aren't just quick fixes; they are a roadmap for lifelong growth. Whether working on personal goals, career advancement, or relationship development, the strategies in this book will equip you with the tools to create enduring change through every area of your life.

Mastering Intentions is an invitation to take control of your life with intention. If you are ready to activate your purpose, amplify your personal power, and lead with lasting impact, this book is for you. You have the power to align your life with your deepest values and to inspire those around you to do the same. You have the power to tell your story—and the world needs to hear it!

Each of these three intentions focuses on ten guiding practices designed to help you master your intentions. Concluding each practice, you will find actions to further your Innerwork and your Teamship. Actions for Innerwork summarize the steps you can take individually to harness your inner power and align your actions with your intentions for personal growth. Actions for Teamship summarize the steps you can take collaboratively to foster a mutually empowering environment with the companions you have chosen to share and shape your life experiences.

Intention One: Activate Your Personal Purpose

Intention One sets up the core practices for mastering intentions. You will learn how to unearth what truly matters to you, activate your intentions in alignment with your values, and foster more intentional relationships.

Practice 1: Articulate Your Personal Purpose

Introduces the concept of discovering and articulating your purpose, helping you align your actions with your core values. You'll explore the impact of self-reflection and vulnerability in owning your life story while learning to integrate your purpose into your personal and professional life. Unique exercises like crafting a personal purpose statement and creating a life journey map will enable you to navigate your life with clarity, resilience, and intention. Ready to lead a life of purpose and authenticity? Your journey starts here.

Practice 2: Activate with Intention

Examines the transformative power of aligning your actions with your deeper intentions rather than rigid metric-specific goals. This practice explores how traditional goal-setting methods can lead to frustration while activating intentions helps foster personal growth. By focusing on how you want to feel and evolve, you'll cultivate inspiration, liberation, and abundance. This approach serves as a personal compass, guiding your decisions with clarity and purpose, leading to a more authentic and fulfilling life. Ready to shift from goals to intentions? This practice shows you how.

Practice 3: Act Purposefully

Explores the transformative impact of relationships and how they shape our personal and professional growth. A Companion Audit framework encourages you to assess your connections—whether with family, friends, colleagues, or life partners—and ask, "Is this serving me?" By manifesting intentional relationships, this practice offers strategies for nurturing supportive connections, setting boundaries, and letting go of those that hinder growth. It is a call to embrace relationships that uplift, inspire, and align with your highest intentions. Ready to audit your companions? This practice will guide you.

Intention Two: Amplify Your Power

Intention Two shifts the focus onto amplifying your personal power. You will learn to transform self-doubt, tap your inner confidence, cultivate a winner's mindset, and manifest your future.

Practice 4: Harness Your Inner Confidence

Focuses on building confidence as a learned skill that grows through deliberate practice, decision-making, and positive self-talk. By identifying and countering negative internal dialogue—referred to as your "Brain Bully"—you will be empowered to transform self-doubt into affirmations of strength and capability. The practice provides actionable exercises to foster resilience, such as practicing self-affirmation, embracing challenges, and owning compliments. Whether facing life's small or significant obstacles, this practice offers a powerful roadmap to cultivating inner confidence and mastering your mindset. Ready to silence your Brain Bully? Start here.

Practice 5: Adopt a Winner's Mindset

Reveals the power of persistence, resilience, and growth through adversity. Through personal stories and actionable strategies, see how setbacks can be opportunities for growth, and how true leadership is built on vulnerability, delegation, and authenticity. The practice outlines how you can build a winner's mindset by embracing challenges, maintaining positivity, and learning from failures. Ready to unlock your full potential and overcome obstacles? This practice will help you take action.

Practice 6: Manifest Your Future

Discover the life-changing practice of manifestation, a practice to help you transform your desires into reality. This practice guides you in harnessing the law of attraction, cultivating unshakable belief, and aligning your actions with your aspirations. Through visualization, consistent focus, and intentional habits, you'll learn how to manifest personal and professional goals. This alignment not only sharpens your focus but also fuels your determination to create the life you envision. Ready to manifest the future you desire? This practice will guide your manifestation practices.

Practice 7: Create Empowering Habits

Empower your success through disciplined routines and strategic habits. This practice reveals how time-blocking, prioritization, and a mastery mindset can accelerate your progress. Track your growth with tools like the Mastery Journal while learning the importance of team collaboration and accountability. It offers actionable steps for delegation, systemization, and financial planning, designed to drive your productivity. Through mastering these habits, you'll create a foundation for sustained personal and professional achievement. Ready to build your success through empowered habits? Your next steps begin with this practice.

Intention Three: Lead with Lasting Impact

Intention Three focuses on leadership—both of yourself and others. You will learn tools and practices of Teamship, leading with authenticity and the power of gratitude, to cultivate a life of purpose and abundance.

Practice 8: Foster Teamship

Unlock the transformative power of Teamship, where collaboration, mutual respect, and shared goals lead to extraordinary results. This practice emphasizes the shift from "I" to "we," showing how high-performing teams are built on unity and purpose. Recognize the five stages of team development—forming, storming, norming, performing, and adjourning—and how to navigate each phase. Learn practical strategies for managing conflict, fostering psychological safety, and maintaining accountability to create an environment where creativity thrives, and every team member feels valued. Ready to unlock the full potential of Teamship? Let this practice be your roadmap.

Practice 9: Lead with Authenticity

Lead with authenticity and vulnerability to forge deeper, more meaningful connections in both your personal and professional life. This practice helps you uncover your unique voice and tell your personal story in a way that inspires others. Discover how storytelling can define your leadership brand, build lasting influence, and empower you to lead with integrity. Embrace the power of authenticity to cultivate trust, drive engagement, and lead with purpose. Ready to lead with your authentic voice? Structure your journey here.

Practice 10: Unlock the Power of Gratitude

Embracing gratitude will transform your life. This practice shows how the daily practice of gratitude can improve your mental health, shift your perspective, and enhance personal growth. Through exercises like writing gratitude letters and reflecting on life's positives, you'll cultivate a habit of appreciation that strengthens relationships and nurtures an abundance mindset. Simple acts of gratitude will ripple positivity into every corner of your life, creating lasting change. Ready to cultivate a mindset of gratitude that transforms your life? This practice will empower your attitude of gratitude.

This book is not just a guide: it is your roadmap to unlocking the full potential of your life by understanding, harnessing, and directing the power of your intentions. Going beyond just achieving goals, it's about creating a life that expresses your deepest values and aspirations. By following these ten proven practices to mastering intentions, you'll activate personal purpose, amplify personal power, and lead with lasting impact.

For further support with mastering your intentions, learn and share more on my website, www.BiancaDAlessio.com, receive my newsletter, and participate in any of my interactive workshops and course modules.

Let's be intentional together!

INTENTION ONE

Activate Your Personal Purpose

Practice 1

ARTICULATE YOUR PERSONAL PURPOSE

*I never recognized my true power until I
started becoming vulnerable.*

Much has been written in recent years on how corporations are leveraging purpose as an animating force for achieving profitable growth. Employees benefit from feeling more connected and aligned with their company's purpose and mission. They also want to grow, have an impact, and make a difference. Similarly, organizations perform at their best when people and teams have clarity and a shared understanding of their goals, enabling them to work in sync to achieve desired business outcomes. This conversation has been extensively documented in the media. Research from McKinsey documents that 70 percent of employees said that their sense of purpose is defined by their work and shows that those who find personal meaning in their work are up to five times more productive than those who don't.[3] Whereas a 2022 Qualtrics study documents that a staggering 52 percent of workers would be willing to take a pay cut to work at a company that has values better aligned with their own.[4] What is new and has recently entered the corporate conversation, however, is how companies can actually help employees discover and activate their personal purpose.

What Do You Want to Be When You Grow Up?

I remember the first time I tried to identify and articulate my "purpose" without an understanding of what I was really being asked to do. I was seventeen years old and applying to college, and while the guidance counselor didn't ask me specifically "What is your personal purpose?" the question "What do you want to do when you graduate from college?" felt the same. If we really think about it, we are posed with this question even earlier in life in the form of "What do you want to be when you grow up?" But how do we even begin to answer that question?

When asked at a young age, it's usually the profession that sounds the "coolest" or has been glamorized by our parents or the media. At five years old, the answer was a doctor because I was sick and wanted to help people feel better. By twelve years old, the answer was to become a lawyer because I had lived through my parents' difficult divorce and thought if I was a

---

[3] Naina Dhingra, Andrew Samo, Bill Schaninger, and Matt Schrimper, "Help your employees find purpose—or watch them leave," McKinsey & Company, April 5, 2021, https://www.mckinsey.com/capabilities/people-and-organizational-performance/our-insights/help-your-employees-find-purpose-or-watch-them-leave.

[4] "Employees who feel aligned with company values are more likely to stay," Qualtrics XM, April 25, 2022, https://www.qualtrics.com/blog/company-values-employee-retention/.

lawyer, I could help families going through what I had lived through. At seventeen years old, the question felt a little less arbitrary and more serious, so the answer was "I have no idea!" And by the time I was nineteen years old, I had just spent a year traveling the world writing a travel blog and therefore wanted to become a travel writer for Condé Nast.

At twenty-three, after graduating college and spending a year working for a nonprofit and traveling around the United States, I was trying to figure out what I would do next. I truly didn't know where to begin: I was hesitant to enter the corporate world because I didn't know where I would fit in or what excited me. What I *did* know was that I loved working with people and being client-facing, I loved problem-solving, I had an eye for detail, and enjoyed exercising the creative side of my brain. I also knew that I wanted to be part of something bigger than myself. Real estate excited me, but I didn't know much about the brokerage space, so, like anything else I knew nothing about, I jumped right in and I started studying to get my license. A few months later I moved back to New York City, passed my licensing exam, began interviewing with brokerage firms, and started working in the industry full-time. I didn't know how it would pan out and had no great big plans or vision for how it would work, I just knew that I needed to start somewhere.

It wasn't until I was twenty-nine years old and a business partnership went sideways that I was forced to start all over again, leading to the formation of my current company—The Masters Division. I finally figured out my purpose—or I thought I had, until a friend of mine told me about an award-winning "Pathway to Purpose" program that changed his life. He shared an exercise with me that helped him locate and articulate his personal purpose. After trying it for myself, I felt like I had clarity for the first time and could finally begin to properly articulate my purpose.

Crafting a Personal Purpose Statement

"Helping people discover something inside them that they don't have the words for" is how Tal Goldhamer, Chief Learning Officer of Ernst & Young (EY), described the desired outcome of EY's award-winning "Pathway to Purpose" program.[5] Ernst & Young (EY), known as one of the "Big Four" accounting firms, helps businesses, governments, and organizations navigate complex challenges, drive innovation, and achieve sustainable growth. In 2020, EY launched a program to assist employees in integrating their personal purpose into their work and lives. The program focused on practices that could significantly impact outcomes for individuals. EY recognized that while many sources discuss personal purpose, few provide guidance on how to identify, articulate, and incorporate personal purpose into one's work and life.

The program offered employees the opportunity to discover and articulate their purpose and encouraged them to align that purpose with various aspects of their lives. It also provided them with a set of words that could serve as a decision-making filter, a series of prompts to guide them to communicate goals and objectives and to use when making decisions to stay in alignment with their purpose. So far, over twenty-five thousand employees have undergone some form of EY's "Pathway

---

[5] "Employees who feel aligned with company values are more likely to stay," Qualtrics XM, April 25, 2022, https://www.qualtrics.com/blog/company-values-employee-retention/.

to Purpose" program and it's had a positive impact on various employee engagement metrics including retention, satisfaction, and happiness. Goldhamer described the program as a journey of self-reflection:

> *"This is not learning in the traditional sense; we're not teaching people knowledge. This program is about self-reflection and helping people discover something inside them that they don't have the words for."*
> —Tal Goldhamer[6]

In one variation of the EY program experienced by a friend of mine, participants begin the facilitated session with story prompts that help them share personal experiences in their life journeys. Example prompts include:

- *When you were young, what did you most love doing? What gave you the most joy?*
- *Describe a particular moment when you felt satisfaction after meeting and overcoming a challenge.*
- *Describe a moment from the past year in your work or personal life when you felt that you were at your best or most proud as an individual or part of a team.*
- *Describe a time when you helped a specific individual after which you felt gratified because you had accomplished something.*

---

[6] Brandon Hall Group, "EY's Chief Learning Officer Talks About Personal Purpose Within Company Vision," GlobeNewswire, May 4, 2022, https://www.globenewswire.com/en/news-release/2022/05/04/2436038/0/en/EY-s-Chief-Learning-Officer-Talks-About-Personal-Purpose-Within-Company-Vision.html.

Fellow participants were asked to actively listen, take notes, and identify key words and ideas from the stories shared. They then shared back to the storytellers the themes they heard, and based on collective observations received about these themes, the storytellers were invited to create and refine several drafts of a personal purpose statement using a specific format:

I am _____ *(name) and my purpose is to* _____ *(insert action) so that* _____ *(insert desired impacts).*

Once articulated, the process from the individual's perspective goes as follows:

First, to state: "This is my purpose, and I deeply believe that it resonates with me. It speaks to me and aligns with my past experiences."

Next, to ask: "How well does this work or activity I'm engaged in align with my purpose?"

If your answer is "a lot," then that's great! It means you're engaging in activities that are aligned with your personal purpose.

If your answer is "a little," then at least you have gained some insight. This may lead to the realization, "Now I understand why I don't feel fulfilled in my life or work." You can then decide what conversations and actions you might wish to undertake to improve the alignment of your efforts with your personal purpose.

Exercise 1.1: Articulating Your Purpose—A New Way to Introduce Yourself

Have you ever thought about introducing yourself based on your purpose rather than your job title? The next time you're invited to introduce yourself, experiment with introducing yourself using your purpose as your descriptor instead of your job and company.

By using EY's formula, this is how I would introduce myself:

> I am Bianca D'Alessio and my purpose is to lead with vulnerability and authenticity so that I can build businesses that prioritize people, their self-development, and their commitment to personal growth and excellence.

Try it! I speculate your post-introduction conversation will be much more exciting and authentic, and your exchange partner will have a much higher assessment of your personal motivation.

The Power of Vulnerable Sharing

The misconception most people have around finding their purpose is that they think that passion is the only driving force to isolate and identify it. The reality is that in order to find passion, and in turn purpose, people must spend years working hard and committing themselves to self-discovery: to not only learn what they're good at, but fully understand who they are and what has shaped them as a person. We all have a life journey and a story we tell about that journey; each of our stories are special and unique—and they are also ours to own and to tell.

For years, I was embarrassed by my story. I had made myself believe that my story made me "less than." I feared that people wouldn't want to work with me if they knew it and that I would never be respected. I convinced myself that I wasn't capable of being in a successful relationship and that I would never be able to amount to more because my story would hold me back from becoming. I was traumatized and embarrassed, and it turned out that keeping my secret—keeping all of my secrets—cost me relationships, business, money, and mental and emotional freedom.

One day a few years ago, I was sitting on the couch of a prospective client in a $12.5 million apartment. She was hammering me with questions about whether I could get her the price she wanted and how long it was going to take for me to get her that number. I could tell during her line of questioning that something was different about this conversation, different from all of the other listing appointments I had gone to: there was extreme pressure, concern, and fear in her voice. I let the conversation continue to flow, and after two hours, we were wrapping up and saying our goodbyes. On our way out, when she left her family behind in the living room and walked me to the door, I said to her, "I just want you to know that whether you decide to work with me or not, I am here for you and I want what is best for your family. But are you okay? Because I understand what it's like to be under severe financial pressure and the paralyzing fear that comes along with feeling like at any point in time you can lose it all."

She asked me how I knew what that feeling felt like.

And there for the first time ever in her entryway, I shared the story of one of the lowest points of my life: it was as raw, honest, and vulnerable as I had ever been. At that point in my career, I no longer would get nervous when I was meeting with and pitching new clients, but I still left that meeting shaking.

I couldn't believe I had just told a potential client that my father was a convicted felon and that I had invested every dollar I had ever made and saved into his real estate deals—so when he got in legal trouble, I lost it all. That I knew what it was like to feel weak and hopeless. That I understood what it was like to have to take care of my family and not have any resources to do so. I knew what it was like to lose everything and have to start all over again, completely terrified and unsure where to start.

She listened and she nodded. I left by saying, "I don't know what your story is. But this is mine. I've never shared this with anyone, but I want you to hear it because when I say I understand what you're going through and that I will help you take care of your family, I mean it, because I've been there and I've had to do it for mine."

The next day she called me, thanked me for sharing my story, and told me she wanted to work with me. For the first time in a long time I felt power: power in self-awareness, power in vulnerability, power in storytelling.

Years later, after finally embracing the discomfort of telling and owning my story, I had the opposite experience.

As I sat with another prospective client I was posed with the question "Have you ever been involved with a lawsuit?" It was a question that used to make my hands clam up and my heart start pounding out of my chest, but now I opened up and shared freely—I had nothing to hide. That was a part of my story; it didn't define me, but it had certainly shaped me. I started sharing.

Her response to my vulnerability was that "sitting next to me made her want to vomit" and then she went on to say that she wished she had someone else present so that I could be "escorted from her property immediately."

I graciously stood up, thanked her for her time, wished her the best of luck and walked out with my pride and dignity intact. I had never been more proud of myself: proud of my honesty, proud of my strength, proud of my vulnerability, and proud of my integrity. Proud that I could use my voice, own my story, and remain authentic no matter the situation. I was just as proud of myself in that moment as I was with the other client when I won the business. Because there I got to experience what most people would consider to be the "worst-case" scenario—losing the business. But for me, by remaining true to my values, my mission, and my passion, it only reaffirmed that no business and no relationship is worth compromising my values or integrity for.

Activating your purpose takes self-awareness, it takes understanding all of the bits and pieces that make you, you. It's about recognizing each of the life experiences and core moments in your life—both the high and low points—that got you to exactly where you are today.

Creating a Life Journey Map

One of my favorite things Tony Robbins has said is "If you're gonna blame people for all the shit, you better blame them for all of the good too. If you're gonna give them credit for everything that's fucked up, then you have to give them credit for everything that's great too."[7] The same goes for the high and the low moments in our lives.

The journey of our life is fluid and rapidly changing. Our lives are filled with experiences that shape who we are today. Some of these experiences lift us up, bringing joy, success,

---

[7] "Tony Robbins! if you're gonna blame people for all the sh**t...," from "Tony Robbins: I Am Not Your Guru," directed by Joe Berlinger, released July 15, 2016, Netflix, clip uploaded by Jeff Arguello, YouTube, January 22, 2017, https://www.youtube.com/watch?v=nqw0FZdQl-k.

and fulfillment—these are the "highs" of our journey. Others challenge us, leading to periods of struggle, loss, or disappointment—these are the "lows." Visualizing and reflecting on these highs and lows provide valuable insights into our growth, resilience, and the patterns that define our lives. The extreme lows that test us and teach us the resilience that leads us to the incredible highs where we get to experience joy and gratitude.

Creating my own "Life Journey Map" helped me visualize the ups and downs of my life to date. By mapping out these significant moments, I gained an increased perspective of how past experiences have shaped my current self and given me the efficacy to navigate future challenges with intention and purpose. This is a powerful tool we can use to tell our stories: by identifying and reflecting on key life events, we can better understand the forces that have shaped our personal and professional journeys to date.

Explicitly recognizing the patterns of recovery and growth after your low points will help you build resilience for future challenges. Additionally, collectively acknowledging both the highs and the lows as integral parts of your Life Journey can help you nurture a balanced perspective on success and setbacks. Powerful global C-suite executives (those senior members of a company whose job titles begin with the letter "C") are trained in this methodology and utilize it individually and with their teams.

Exercise 1.2: Life Journey Map

This exercise will help you create a visual representation of your life's highs and lows across five Life Stages:

1) **Formative Years (<17 years old):** Early life experiences shaped primarily by family, education, and childhood friends.
2) **Young Adult Years (18–21 years old):** Pursuing knowledge, forming more mature relationships, and first career choices.
3) **Early Career Years (22–29 years old):** Establishing professional identity, building networks, and navigating adult relationships.
4) **Mid-Career Years (30–39 years old):** Professional choices, milestones, team and leadership roles, personal life choices, and increased responsibilities for others.
5) **Late Career Years (40+ years old):** Professional choices, milestones, team and leadership roles, expanded personal life choices and greater responsibilities, including more community engagement.

Start by setting up your graph: Draw a horizontal line across the middle of a piece of paper. This is your baseline, the neutral point that will represent the timeline of your life starting from your earliest foundational event on the left to the present day on the right. Everything above the line will represent positive life events (highs), and below the line will represent negative life events (lows).

Depending on your age, draw three to five vertical lines equally spaced to separate the Life Stages as defined above: formative, young adult, early career, mid-career, and late career, and then identify the key life events by stage (both highs and lows). Reflecting on your life chronologically, identify significant moments that stand out as either highs or lows. These could be personal achievements, relationships, career milestones, losses, challenges, or other impactful experiences.

Consider the emotional impact and importance of each event, as not every high or low is equal to other highs and lows in your life. It's important to begin charting these key moments in your life to signal how significant they've been by changing the line distance from the baseline: your highest high should have the longest line towards the top of the page and your lowest low should have the longest line towards the bottom of the page. Label each line as you start charting and include the age at which the event happened in brackets.

At the end you might end up with a Life Journey Map that looks similar to mine:

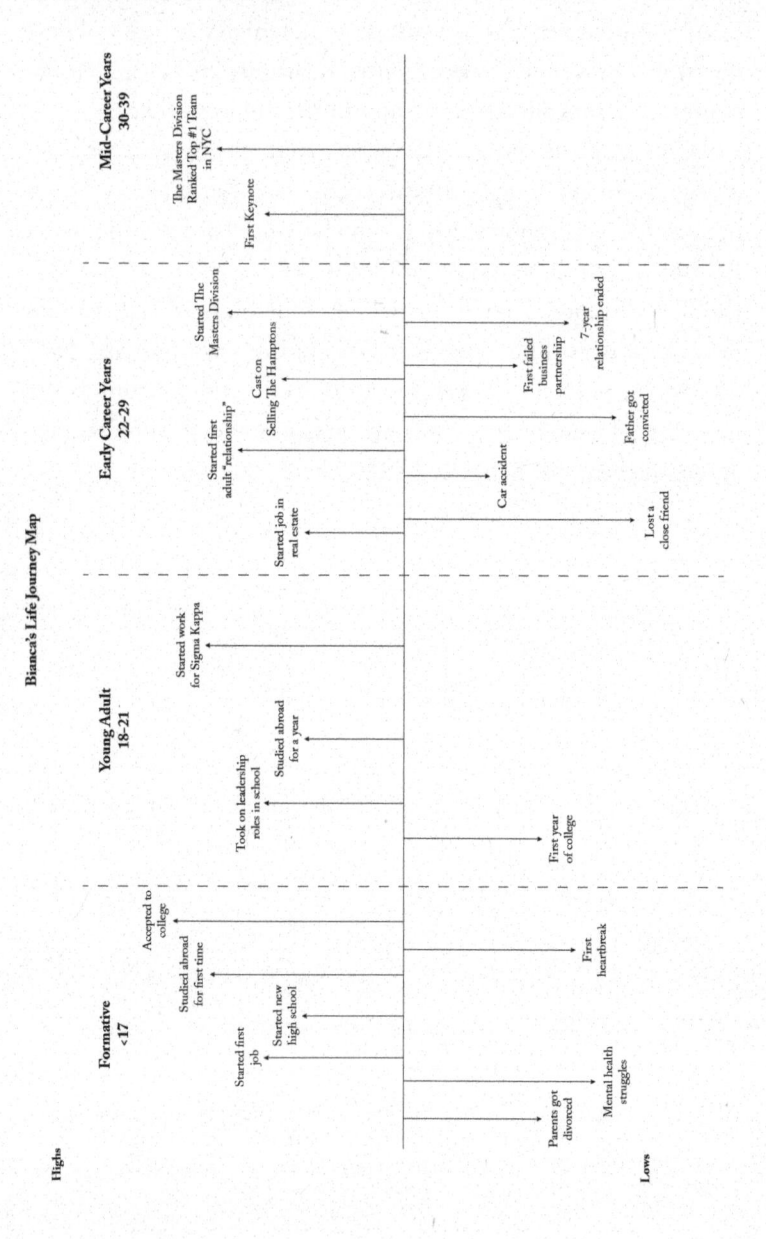

Bianca's Life Journey Map

Formative <17	Young Adult 18-21	Early Career Years 22-29	Mid-Career Years 30-39

Highs:
- Started first job
- Studied abroad for first time
- Accepted to college
- Started new high school
- Took on leadership roles in school
- Studied abroad for a year
- Started work for Sigma Kappa
- Started job in real estate
- Started first adult "relationship"
- Cast on Selling The Hamptons
- Started The Masters Division
- First Keynote
- The Masters Division Ranked Top #1 Team in NYC

Lows:
- Parents got divorced
- Mental health struggles
- First heartbreak
- First year of college
- Lost a close friend
- Car accident
- Father got convicted
- First failed business partnership
- 7-year relationship ended

MASTERING INTENTIONS

This is an opportunity for creativity; represent the journey your way. I've seen some people represent a windy road with each bend in the road representing a milestone while others have used miniature pictures and graphics instead of words as props to tell their stories.

Life Journey Map

	Formative <17	Young Adult 18–21	Early Career Years 22–29	Mid-Career Years 30–39	Late Career Years 40+
Highs					
Lows					

Now that you've completed your chart, step back and reflect on the overall patterns of your Life Journey Map. Ask yourself:

1) What do the highs and lows reveal about my life's trajectory?
2) Are there any patterns in how I experience or recover from lows?
3) How have the highs shaped my sense of purpose and direction?
4) What lessons have I learned from both the highs and the lows?

When I created my own Life Journey Map, I realized that each of my lowest lows was the catalyst that allowed me to achieve my next breakthrough high. The lows became stepping stones for moments of tremendous growth. When I look at my Life Journey Map, I feel powerful because I'm able to go back to crucial moments and access the memories of when those things happened. I remember what I was able to overcome and how hard it was to pull myself out of those deep moments of despair, and I feel a sense of confidence and relief knowing each of those moments of pain were temporary and that things always get better. Sometimes it takes much longer for life to turn around, but this tool helped me realize that, while I'm not in control of the event that has occurred, I am in full control of how it changed my life perspective and how I respond to and grow from the event.

Another key takeaway from this exercise is to recognize your resilience—because you are resilient and you have overcome hard things. When I go through difficult times now, I often put myself back exactly where I was during one of my low points knowing the experience and the situation isn't the same. I find strength knowing that I have overcome something in the past and, therefore, can do it again. Resilience can be built through muscle memory. The best entrepreneurs, leaders, and changemakers are not only resilient, but are also able to bounce back from adversity very quickly. *A Setback is a Setup for a Comeback*[8] is a catchphrase and book title by motivational speaker Willie Jolley that I feel wonderfully encapsulates this idea of bouncing back, but to create that comeback muscle memory takes conscious effort and tremendous self-awareness.

Using this Exercise in Your Personal Life

While I encourage you to complete this exercise individually for the first time, it can also be a powerful tool to do and share with your family, including siblings, parents, children, and partners. Personally, this tool has allowed me to create a deeper connection with my family through examining my parents' divorce. In fact, on each of my sibling's—as well as my parents'—Life Journey Maps, the divorce is a low point for all five of us. However, it has impacted us all very differently and has varying significance to each person in my family. For me, I struggled with depression for many, many years following my parents' divorce. However, my brother and sister, who were much younger when they divorced, had a very different experience. That isn't to say it was less significant or didn't impact them later in life, but in their charts the experience was felt many years later, while for me it had an almost immediate impact. Do you see how the same exact experience can have tremendously different impacts on people at different stages of life?

---

[8] Willie Jolley, *A Setback is a Setup for a Comeback* (New York City: St. Martin's Press, 2000).

Ultimately, by doing the inner work and reflecting, you can use this chart as a platform and opportunity to begin having conversations with the companions in your life in order to build more meaningful connections and deeper relationships.

Using this Exercise in a Professional Setting

The Life Journey Map can also have immense value within organizations and teams. When utilized in a professional environment, this can become a powerful tool for building trust, empathy, and cohesion within a team. The objective is to enhance team dynamics and mutual understanding. By sharing and visually mapping out your individual and collective life experiences, your team can develop a deeper understanding of each other, enhancing collaboration and mutual support.

Organizations that recognize that our personal lives have a significant impact on our professional contributions have employees and leaders who become much more connected to the organization and its people. Research by BetterUp documents that fostering workplace belonging leads to a 56 percent increase in job performance and a 50 percent reduction in turnover risk. Employees who feel connected to their peers also experience a 75 percent reduction in sick days.[9] In short, organizations have more high-performing individuals and stronger retention rates because their people feel supported by the company and its employees.

---

[9] "The Value of Belonging at Work: New Frontiers for Inclusion in 2021 and Beyond," Better Up, accessed July 25, 2024, https://grow.betterup.com/resources/the-value-of-belonging-at-work-the-business-case-for-investing-in-workplace-inclusion.

In the professional setting, the Life Journey Map exercise is designed to help teams explore their collective highs and lows, creating a shared narrative that enhances team dynamics and mutual understanding. Seeing as teams are composed of individuals with unique life experiences that shape their perspectives, strengths, and contributions to the group, understanding and appreciating each other's life journeys can foster deeper connections, empathy, and collaboration within the team. Ultimately, this exercise can be employed to help your team navigate and learn from its collective highs and lows, as well as an opportunity to strengthen its foundational readiness for future challenges and successes together. It will also foster open and honest dialogue about individual journeys and how they influence the team's dynamics, improving trust and communication. Sharing narratives helps highlight the reservoirs of strength and resilience of the team, both individually and collectively.

When conducted in an organization, I recommend this activity be led in small groups with someone guiding the activity as well as the conversation and questions that follow.

Facilitating the Team Journey Map

Request each member of the team to individually reflect in silence on their respective life journeys. Give them fifteen minutes to work on their own charts, asking them to consider the emotional impact and importance of each event.

Creating an opportunity and safe space in an organization to be vulnerable with coworkers requires comfort and trust. In order to create that space, the moderator should begin by sharing their own Life Journey Map with the group, then invite each team member to share their identified highs and lows.

Prior to sharing, the moderator should ask the group to be respectful and actively listen as each person shares.

Exercise 1.3: Active Listening

Exercises such as this are a great opportunity to practice active listening, another powerful relationship skill. The key components for active listening are:

- **Give Full Attention:** The speaker should have full attention without interruption or distraction.
- **Use Body Language:** Show you are listening by making eye contact with the speaker and engaging with their story. Leaning in, smiling, and nodding are signs that you are actively listening. Avoid negative facial expressions.
- **Be Empathetic:** There can be triggers and traumas that are brought up during this exercise that may impact others in the room. Be empathetic of each person's different experiences and refrain from passing judgment.

As each member shares, they should briefly explain the significance of each event and how it has shaped them. The sharing should be respectful, with team members actively listening without interrupting.

Once completed, facilitate some of these questions with the team:

1) What do the shared highs and lows reveal about your team's collective experiences?
2) How do individual experiences influence your team's dynamics, strengths, and challenges?

3) Are there common themes or patterns across your team members' journeys?
4) During your lows, do you tend to withdraw and become less engaged or do you find more connection and meaning through you and your coworkers' work during those difficult times?
5) How could understanding each other's highs and lows improve this team's collaboration and support?
6) How has your personal resilience made you a better leader or coworker?
7) What actions could we take to support each other's growth and resilience, both individually and as a team?

By having a deeper understanding of our team members' life journeys, you can build deeper connections and a stronger collective resilience for the team. Conclude the exercise by reflecting on the process as a team, asking:

1) How did it feel to share my personal highs and lows with my team?
2) What did I learn about my teammates that I didn't know before?

The strength of any team lies not just in its collective achievements, but also in how they navigate and learn from their collective highs and lows. Take a minute of silence to acknowledge each other's vulnerabilities that were shared during this exercise.

Reflect deeply and honestly, knowing that each point on your map is a stepping stone on the path to your personal growth and self-awareness. By acknowledging the highs and lows, you can better appreciate the experiences that have shaped you and better prepare for the road ahead. Mastering your intentions requires embracing the full spectrum of your journey—learning from the lows and celebrating the highs!

When I conducted this with my leadership team, it unveiled far more than I anticipated. By individually reflecting on the growth of the company and the pivotal moments we experienced together, my employees were not only able to see how they impacted business functions, but how it transformed them as leaders and in their positions. It affirmed that the high moments created waves of momentum that we were all able to ride in order to reach the next height in business. More importantly, it unearthed conversations about how the low moments impacted my employees personally; how it challenged them both inside and outside of the office. It brought up conversations about how it affected their personal relationships, but also how they were able to learn about themselves, become stronger leaders, and become better companions in their personal lives. It showed everyone that the work we do in our office doesn't just stay within our four walls: it seeps into everything. By leaning into these moments of growth, we could enhance our relationships and our experiences in all aspects of our lives.

Summary of Practice 1: Articulate Your Personal Purpose

In order to be able to articulate your personal purpose, you must first understand and own your life story. Personal purpose isn't just a buzzword; it's the key to unlocking clarity, fulfillment, and intentionality in your life and work. By reflecting on your experiences—the highs and the lows—you gain insights into what drives you and how those experiences have shaped you.

Self-reflection and vulnerability will be common themes in this book, but the journey starts here. By creating a personal purpose statement and mapping out the pivotal moments in your life, you'll begin to see patterns, build resilience, and step into your own purpose with greater intention. Whether in your personal life or professional setting, owning your purpose is the foundation for creating a life of impact and meaning.

Implications for Innerwork

- Reflect deeply on your life story to unearth your personal purpose.
- Create a personal purpose statement that aligns with your values and life experiences.
- Use your personal purpose as a decision-making filter to align your actions.
- Introduce yourself by your purpose instead of job title to foster more meaningful connections.
- Appreciate both highs and lows to contribute to your personal growth.

Implications for Teamwork

- Encourage team members to shape their personal purpose.
- Facilitate opportunities for team members to introduce themselves based on their purpose.
- Organize sessions where team members can share their life highs and lows to build team cohesion and mutual support.

- Create a safe space to share Life Journey Maps, fostering vulnerability and authenticity.
- Ensure that all team members are trained in the practice of active listening.

Practice 2

ACTIVATE WITH INTENTION

Commit yourself every day to becoming the best version of yourself.

American philosopher Charles Scott refers to the concept of the "middle voice."[10] The middle voice represents actions that we perform on ourselves, actions where we're both the doer and the receiver. In leadership and life, embracing the middle voice means recognizing that we're both the *architect* of our actions and the *beneficiary* of their outcomes. Our actions are deeply intertwined with our personal growth. When we invest in ourselves—whether by developing new skills, building resilience, or nurturing relationships—we're not just achieving external success, we're also intentionally shaping the person we will become.

---

[10] Charles E. Scott, "The Middle Voice of Metaphysics," *The Review of Metaphysics* 42, no. 4 (1989): 743-764, accessed July 29,2024, https://www.pdcnet.org/revmetaph/content/revmetaph_1989_0042_0004_0743_0764.

Something big and very transformative happened to me a few years ago when I changed the way I was setting my goals. I used to be very, very rigid with my New Year's resolutions. Prior to changing my practice, every December I made a list of the things I wanted to accomplish. At the midyear point, I made it a habit to check in on them. Near the end of the year, I would again see if I was still on track.

For over a decade, I was in a never-ending loop of goal setting and experiencing disappointment when I wouldn't live up to the standard I wanted to set for myself. I felt like I was on this hamster wheel, constantly feeling like everything I was doing was "never enough" (a feeling many high performers, entrepreneurs, and business owners experience). I was becoming burntout by my own self-imposed expectations. Something needed to change—I needed to make a change.

Quit Setting Toxic, Metric-Specific Goals

One of the key foundations I'd been taught when it came to setting goals was that they should be measurable, and mine were very metric-specific. I made goals like how much weight I wanted to lose, how much money I wanted to make, how many days I wanted to exercise, and how many places I wanted to travel to. While this practice kept me moving in the right direction towards my "ultimate" goals, it also led me to become hypercritical of myself based on my performance. I became so rigid in working towards hitting these specific goals, that there became very little room for other growth opportunities. I was becoming narrow-minded and blindsided to other things that existed. I also lost my *why*: why did these goals matter? Why did that number mean anything? Would it really make me happier if I lost ten pounds this year? Would I feel better about myself if I doubled my savings from last year to this year? The answer would be yes to both, but why that number? Would I feel like a failure if I lost eight pounds instead of ten? Would I be disappointed if I saved more money than last year but not the multiple that I had listed on a piece of paper?

In the hustle and bustle of daily life, it's easy to lose sight of what truly matters to us and continue toxic practices. We often get caught up in the immediate demands of our careers, personal lives, and obligations, leaving little time for reflection on our deeper intentions and goals. On December 31, 2022, I was sitting in my office reviewing my New Year's resolutions from years past. I had the handwritten pieces of paper that I wrote my goals on from 2015 through 2022, and at the end of each year I would record my progress next to each goal.

I'd been influenced by the concept of SMART Goals. SMART stands for Specific, Measurable, Achievable, Relevant, and Time-bound. These serve as parameters to ensure your objectives are attainable within a certain time period. In my mind, I thought I was doing the "right thing" by utilizing this practice. As I was staring at these papers in front of me, I realized that I had actually created a platform to be self-critical of myself, a soap box for my Brain Bully (we'll talk more about this in Practice 4). I was trying to apply a corporate concept to my personal growth that was too rigid and singularly focused. While SMART goals have an incredible use and function—at times—in my personal arena, this method of goal setting wasn't serving me.

The reality was that a year into starting my business, a business that had grown way faster than I expected, I was exceeding all expectations I'd set for myself. From the outside in, things looked amazing—and from a goals perspective, I was achieving them all—but from a personal perspective, I was so stressed I couldn't sleep anymore; I was so busy moving through the motions I felt completely uninspired, stopped taking care of myself, and was watching day after day as my health declined. I didn't want to be that person anymore; I wasn't proud of that person. She'd accomplished all of the "things," but she wasn't a woman I respected or who I wanted to be. So, I changed my approach. Instead of chasing the SMART goal, I knew I needed to shift my energy into becoming the person who was capable of achieving those SMART goals.

Focus on the Feeling, Not the Result

I scraped my New Year's resolutions and instead established a new practice of "Activating Intentions." I've been using this practice (which I subsequently came to learn was based on activating my middle voice) ever since with very positive results. Instead of setting rigid, metric-specific goals, I now focus on how I want to feel by the end of the year. I begin by identifying three key feelings and intentions I want to cultivate to shape the person I wish to become. I first ask myself "Where am I lacking in my life right now?" Then I pose the question: "What are the three things that I want to feel at the end of the year in my relationships, in my work, in my purpose, and in my extracurricular activities?" From there I intentionally align my actions with those desired feelings. As a result, I find that I can now create ongoing outcomes that are productive and fulfilling to me. Ultimately, doing this exercise serves as my personal compass for the year: it empowers me to take greater control of my life, ensuring that my actions are in harmony with my values and aspirations.

Always Three Things, Always Evolving

My three things vary by design; they're moving targets. After all, life is about the evolution of personal growth and self-discovery.

In 2023, I was rapidly moving the business through its supergrowth stage, not paying attention to my health or the pleasures outside of work that brought me joy. My relationships were suffering, I was losing myself, and I became so bogged down by the daily operations that I lost sight of the big picture. I felt lost and needed to make a change. I began my Activating Intentions practice, and my three words for the year became Inspired, Liberated, and Abundant.

Inspired

I wanted to feel inspired by the work I was doing and the people in my life. So, before I took on new business or worked with new clients, I would ask myself, "Does this work inspire me?" Additionally, I changed my hiring practice. After interviewing new people to join my company, instead of focusing on if I felt they were right or wrong for the role, I asked myself, "Does this person inspire me? Am I inspired by their story? Am I inspired by their work ethic? Am I inspired by their passion, excitement, and enthusiasm?" If I am inspired by them and they are a person I want to be around, I will find the right role and position for them in my organization because I will want to grow with and around them. And I knew that if I was going to level up, I needed to be inspired by the people I was learning from. This brought me back to one of my favorite quotes from Jim Rohn: "You are the average of the five people you spend the most time with."[11] So I started looking for this group of people: those who were smarter than me, more successful than me, and wealthier than me. In short, people who I could learn from to help me become better.

Liberated

I missed feeling freedom, so I began to focus on liberation. I was working over twenty hours a day and had no social life and no hobbies. I remember thinking to myself that I used to be such an interesting person and all of a sudden I found myself with nothing else to talk about besides work, which resulted in me pulling away from anyone who wasn't in my work sphere, like my family and friends. I felt like I couldn't relate to the most important people in the world to me anymore. I needed to make a change before I would really lose myself and the people who mattered most to me. So, I went back to doing things I loved and exploring new hobbies. I began dancing, started traveling again, and, in time, I felt excitement and energy in the activities that brought me joy, instead of just finding joy through professional successes alone.

---

[11] Jim Rohn, "Quote by Jim Rohn: 'You are the average of the five people you spend the most time with.'" Goodreads, accessed June 15, 2024, https://www.goodreads.com/quotes/1798-you-are-the-average-of-the-five-people-you-spend.

Abundant

I wanted to know that I was capable of being more than just good at any one thing at a time. I didn't just want to build a great business, I also wanted to be a great person, an incredible sister, a caring daughter, and a deserving partner. I wanted abundance. So, I shifted my perspective and began leading with an abundance mindset, believing that anything I wanted to achieve, I would be able to if I put in the hard work and had the discipline. From there, an abundance of love, joy, success, freedom, and gratitude would follow.

Taking this exercise seriously meant taking more control of my life. It encouraged me to engage in a proactive, intentional approach to my personal and professional growth. Today, I keep my current set of three intentions at the forefront of my decision-making. For every major decision, I ask myself "Does this align with my three intentions for the year?"

This practice has also become one of living intentionally, encouraging me to pause, reflect, and realign with my true self. It helps me identify and articulate my intentions for the year ahead, aligning my actions with the feelings and outcomes I want to achieve. The purpose of Activating Intentions is to help you identify and articulate your core intentions for the year, aligning your actions with the feelings and outcomes you want to experience in your relationships, work, purpose, and extracurricular activities. By completing the exercise, you will create a clear and actionable framework to guide your decision-making throughout the year. As you prepare to lead in various capacities, I know from experience that this exercise will help you develop the self-awareness and emotional intelligence necessary for you to navigate the complexities of your personal leadership journey with grace and authenticity. Embrace this exercise as a tool for transformation and experience how it helps you create the life you truly desire, as it has done for me.

Exercise 2.1: Activating Intentions

Now it's your turn. This exercise can activate you to be the architect of your own experience, ensuring that your year is guided by purpose, clarity, and a strong sense of self. Personally, it helps me create a clear and actionable framework to guide my decision-making throughout the year. Here is how you do it:

1) **Reflect on Your Current State**
   a) Reflect on the following question: *"Where am I lacking in my life right now?"*
   b) Consider all aspects of your life—your relationships, work, personal growth, and extracurricular activities.
   c) Document these thoughts, focusing on areas where you feel unfulfilled, disconnected, or in need of improvement.
2) **Specify Three Desired Feelings**
   a) Ask yourself: *"What are the three things that I want to feel at the end of the year in my relationships, in my work, in my purpose, and in my extracurricular activities?"*
   b) Consider the feelings that resonate most deeply with you. These might include discipline, gratitude, abundance, connection, fulfillment, joy, or peace.
   c) Write down three key feelings or intentions that if you felt that feeling it would impact every

other component of your life (relationships, work, purpose, extracurricular activities, and so on). Be specific and choose words that truly capture the essence of what you want to experience.

3) **Articulate Your Intentions**
   a) For each key feeling or intention, write a brief statement that encapsulates how you want to embody this feeling in your daily life. For example:
      i) *"I will cultivate discipline in my work by setting clear goals and following through with consistent action."*
      ii) *"I will foster gratitude in my relationships by expressing appreciation regularly to those I care about."*
      iii) *"I will embrace abundance in my purpose by recognizing and valuing the opportunities that come my way."*
   b) Make sure your statements are positive, actionable, and reflective of your true desires.

4) **Activate through Actions**
   a) Consider how you can integrate these into your daily life.
   b) Ask yourself the following question before making any major decisions or commitments: *"Does this align with the three main things that I want to feel this year?"*
   c) If the decision supports your intentions, proceed with confidence; if not, reconsider your approach or seek alternatives that align better with your desired outcomes.

5) **Review and Adjust**
    a) Every three months, set aside time to revisit your intentions and reflect on your progress. Ask yourself:
        i) *Am I feeling these three things?*
        ii) *Am I consistently aligning my actions with my intentions? What adjustments do I need to make to stay on track?*
        iii) *Does this relationship and this goal that I'm setting for myself align with the three main things that I want to feel?*
    b) Don't be afraid to revise your intentions if your circumstances or priorities change. The goal is to stay true to what feels right for you at any given time.

6) **Commit to the Practice**
    a) Consistency is critical to making this exercise effective. Commit to using this exercise as a guiding framework throughout the year.
    b) Share your intentions with a trusted friend or mentor who can provide support and accountability.
    c) Consider keeping a journal to document your reflections, decisions, and experiences as you align your actions with your intentions (I say *consider* because while I don't yet do this, I understand how this step could add value to this exercise).

Identifying My Core Values

Graduating students are frequently presented with the Dr. Seuss book *Oh, the Places You'll Go!*[12] The inspiring message within the illustrated cartoon book encourages readers to find the success that lies within, no matter what challenges they face.

Irish Philosopher Samuel Beckett wrote a more complex version that reverberates more deeply with me and really helps me open up to new possibilities and stretch goals:

> *"Where would I go, if I could go,*
> *who would I be, if I could be,*
> *what would I say if I had a voice,*
> *who says this, saying it's me?"*[13]

These four questions by Beckett are deeply relevant to me today in shaping my aspiration to be a reflective and intentional leader. Let's take a closer look at each now:

"Where would I go, if I could go?" invites us to reflect and articulate our intention for ourselves. In our lives, and especially in how we choose to lead, we often find ourselves at a crossroads, wondering about the paths we could take. These choices shape our internal identity—who we become as leaders and individuals as well as our external circumstances. Beckett's first question invites contemplation of our choices.

"Who would I be, if I could be?" invites us to reflect on the nature of our true selves. What is the ideal version of who we aspire to be? This question is a reminder that we need to

---

[12] Dr. Seuss, *Oh, the Places You'll Go!* (New York City: Random House Books for Young Readers, 1990).

[13] Samuel Beckett, *Stories and Texts for Nothing* (New York City: Grove Press, 1966).

contemplate our possibilities about who we could be. We don't spend as much time as we should future casting our possibilities.

"What would I say if I had a voice?" Here, we are invited to consider the power of our voice to communicate our values and intentions. In leadership, our voice is our tool for influence. Our voice carries weight; it influences and inspires others, ensuring that what we say and do reflects our core beliefs and intentions. Talking at conferences, posting my thoughts on social media, and writing this book are various ways I have chosen to exercise my voice. I think about what I want to say and say it. Sometimes it's personal, sometimes inspirational, other times raw. Every time, I feel I am exercising my voice to contribute to the thoughts of others.

"Who says this, saying it's me?" Now Beckett brings us to a fundamental question of identity: who is the "I" that speaks? Who is the true self behind our thoughts and actions? Understanding this is crucial. Beckett reminds us that our actions should align with our values. The root of this alignment is self-awareness and authenticity. This speaks to the essence of leadership—embracing the complexities of life while continuing to move forward, to live, and to lead with honesty and authenticity.

As you reflect on Beckett's words, take time to ask yourself: *Where am I going? Who am I becoming? What am I saying?* Use these questions to guide you to lead with a deeper sense of purpose and intention. By doing so, you will not only navigate your own path with clarity, but you'll also inspire and guide others to do the same. We must confront the aspects of our identity that we might neglect in our busy lives—the doubts, the fears, the dreams that we often push aside. By acknowledging these elements, we can lead more authentically and with greater self-awareness.

This book is my response to these four questions. This is my voice. These are my aspirations. It is my vulnerability on display, and my story as I tell it. This is who I am.

The Foundation of Intentional Leadership

Understanding and distinguishing between aspirations, values, and norms is not just an intellectual exercise; it's a practical tool for building strong, cohesive, and purpose-driven teams. As leaders, your ability to guide these discussions and ensure that your team is aligned on these elements will set the foundation for intentional and impactful leadership.

Aspirations, Values, and Norms are three fundamental concepts that lie at the heart of effective, intentional leadership. Understanding and distinguishing between these elements is crucial not only for your personal growth as a leader, but also for creating a cohesive, purpose-driven team. Engaging in a team dialogue to clearly define these aspects is a powerful exercise that can transform your leadership approach and strengthen your team's unity.

Before I dive into the distinctions, let's first define what I mean by Aspirations, Values, and Norms.

Aspirations

Aspirations are our dreams and goals for the future. They represent what we hope to achieve or become, both individually and as a team. Aspirations are forward-looking and inspire action toward a desired future state. Aspirations are crucial because they provide motivation and a sense of purpose. They help us and our team stay focused on the future and align our efforts toward a common goal. For instance, if our team aspires to be the leader in sustainable business practices, this aspiration will shape our strategic decisions and actions, pushing us to innovate and set climate benchmarks in our industry.

The clearest example I can provide is the experience of a colleague of mine when he was leading a committee for a Boston-based Babson College alumni group. During their first meeting, the committee members brainstormed the group's aspiration and settled on: "To curate a local alumni community motivated to gather, connect, and learn together." The facilitator, Kevin Mulcahy, a Babson College faculty member, brought this exercise one step further by leading the group through an individual aspiration exercise. He separated the group into pairs and asked each pair to take turns asking the following questions of their partner, three times in succession, using the following format and taking no longer than three minutes each to complete the exercise:

> Person A: What's your goal for being on this team and why are you really here?
>
> Person B: ...*provided their perspective*
>
> Person A: Thank you, now why are you really here?
>
> Person B: ...*provided their perspective*
>
> Person A: Thank you, now why are you really here?
>
> Person B: ...*provided their perspective*

When the exercise was completed, they discussed their responses and each person shared what they'd learned about why the other person was really there.

The result of the exercise was startling to all. In the space of fifteen minutes, Kevin shared that they'd cut through to the key reason of why each of them had volunteered to serve on the committee. All agreed that, to their surprise, they more clearly understood each other's motivations for being on the committee, too.

Values

Values are the core principles and beliefs that guide our behavior and decision-making as we pursue our aspirations. They're the standards by which we judge what's right or wrong, important or unimportant. Values are deeply rooted and serve as a moral compass for both individuals and teams. When faced with a tough choice, referring back to our core values can provide clarity and direction. This is why it's essential for teams to have a clear understanding of their shared values; it ensures that everyone is on the same page and working towards the same ethical standards.

Using the same alumni group committee meeting example, in order to establish and expose the groups shared values, the question was posed "How do we want to work together? What three key values do you believe are critical for us to uphold throughout?"

The group agreed on the following values to guide their work together and posted these on the wall for each committee meeting to ensure they were operating according to the values that they all signed up for:

- Engaging in open debate
- Ensuring equal participation
- Having fun
- Being punctual
- Giving others the benefit of the doubt

Norms

Norms are the shared expectations and rules that guide how members of a group interact with each other. They dictate acceptable behavior within a group and help establish a sense of predictability and order. Norms can be explicit, like official policies, but more commonly are implicit unspoken rules or expectations that govern how team members interact with one another. Norms help create a predictable and stable environment where everyone knows what's expected of them. They're behavioral guidelines that emerge from our values and aspirations. For example, a team might establish a norm of open communications, where everyone is encouraged to share their ideas and feedback without fear of judgment. This norm supports the value of respect and the aspiration to create an inclusive and innovative team culture.

Carrying forward with the alumni group example, the committee members found it particularly productive to answer the following questions:

- How will we make decisions?
- How will we schedule and run our meetings?
- How will we assign responsibilities and follow-through on our commitments?
- What are our expectations for meeting preparation?

- What are our expectations for meeting attendance?

The actual answers are less important to share than the structure of the conversation around establishing norms. Norms are essential for maintaining a cohesive team dynamic because they provide a framework for behavior that helps prevent misunderstandings and conflicts.

The Power of Collective Input: Why This Exercise Matters

When a team takes the time to discuss and agree on their collective aspirations, values, and norms, it creates alignment and unity. Everyone understands the direction in which the team is headed (Aspirations), the principles guiding their actions (Values), and the behaviors expected of them (Norms). This alignment minimizes conflicts, as decisions are made based on a shared understanding of what the team stands for and aims to achieve.

Engaging in this exercise also builds trust within the team. When team members have a say in defining their shared aspirations, values, and norms, they feel a greater sense of ownership and commitment. This sense of ownership fosters a culture of trust, where team members are more likely to support one another and work collaboratively towards common goals.

When complex situations arise in which there are differing opinions, referring back to the team's core values and norms ensures that decisions are made with integrity and consistency. This not only strengthens the team's internal coherence, but also enhances its external reputation.

When a team is clear about its aspirations, values, and norms, it becomes more adaptable and resilient. In times of change or crisis, these elements serve as anchors that keep the team grounded and focused. The team can navigate challenges more effectively because everyone knows what they are working towards and the principles that guide them.

Finally, this exercise empowers and motivates team members. When people are involved in shaping the team's direction and culture, they're more motivated to contribute and take initiative. They see their work as meaningful and aligned with their personal and professional values, which boosts engagement and satisfaction.

Exercise 2.2: Aspirations, Values and Norms

Facilitating a discussion on aspirations, values, and norms can be a transformative experience for any team. Here's how to guide this conversation effectively:

> **Start with Aspirations:** Begin the discussion by asking the team to envision their ideal future. What do they want to achieve together? Encourage them to think big and be ambitious. Write down all ideas and then refine them to a few core aspirations that resonate with everyone.
>
> **Define Values:** Next, move on to values. Ask the team what principles they believe should guide their work and interactions. The key question is: what do we believe are critical for our group to uphold throughout our time

working together? This might include values like integrity, respect, innovation, or collaboration. Discuss why each value is important and how it aligns with the team's aspirations.

Establish Norms: Finally, discuss the norms that will support the team's values and aspirations. What behaviors are necessary to create the environment we want? As a group, what guidelines will govern how we'll work together? This might include norms around communication, decision-making, or conflict resolution. Here are some possible questions you can pose:

- How will we make decisions?
- How will we schedule and run our meetings?
- How will we assign responsibilities and follow through on our commitments?
- What are our expectations for meeting preparation?
- What are our expectations for meeting attendance?
- How will we manage the conversation to promote everyone's learning?

Document and Review: Once the discussion is complete, document the team's agreed upon aspirations, values, and norms. Review them regularly to ensure they remain relevant and continue to guide the team effectively.

Understanding and distinguishing between aspirations, values, and norms is not just an intellectual exercise, it's a practical tool for building strong, cohesive, and purpose-driven teams. As leaders, your ability to guide these discussions and ensure that your team is aligned on these elements will set the foundation for intentional and impactful leadership.

Take this exercise seriously and encourage your team members to do the same. The clarity and unity they bring will enhance your team's performance and foster a work environment where everyone feels valued, motivated, and connected to a larger purpose. Ultimately, by anchoring your leadership in well-defined aspirations, values, and norms, you'll be better equipped to lead with authenticity, integrity, and intention.

Play the Long Game

"One hand for oneself and one for the ship" was the advice given to sea captains to take continual steps to ensure personal well-being in addition to focusing on one's duties or responsibilities on the job. In other words: embrace the long game in every aspect of your life. Keep your eyes on the horizon, stay true to your intentions, and trust that your consistent efforts will lead to lasting success.

Remember, the long game isn't about the sprint, it's about the marathon. It's not about winning today, it's about building a legacy that will endure for years to come. Act in a way today that your future self will thank you for. The long game is about foresight and commitment. It's about aligning your daily actions with your larger goals, even when those goals seem far off. It requires us to see beyond the immediate and to trust that our consistent efforts will pay off over time.

In a world where instant gratification is often the norm, the idea of long-term thinking can feel both challenging and countercultural. We're conditioned to seek quick wins, fast results, and immediate feedback. Yet, the most meaningful successes, both personally and professionally, often require sustained effort, patience, and resilience. This is the essence of the long game—strategically investing in your future, even when the rewards are not immediate.

In Teamship, playing the long game means making decisions that might not yield instant results, but are aligned with your core values and long-term objectives. It's about building relationships, developing skills, and creating systems that will serve you and your organization well into the future. This isn't only about professional growth, it's about personal development too. It's about becoming the kind of person who can *sustain* success, not just achieve it.

The Role of Intentionality

Intentionality is at the heart of the long game. To play the long game effectively, you must first be clear about your intentions. What do you truly want to achieve? What kind of leader do you aspire to be? What values will guide your journey? Intentionality involves aligning your actions with these aspirations. It's about making choices that reflect your long-term goals, even when those choices are difficult or unpopular. It's about staying true to your purpose, even when the path is uncertain.

The Importance of Staying Power

Playing the long game requires more than just vision and intention—it requires action and staying power. Staying power is the resilience to keep going when the road gets tough, the discipline to stay focused amidst distractions, and the perseverance to push through setbacks and challenges. Staying power is what separates those who merely start strong from those who finish strong. It's what allows you to maintain momentum over the long haul, even when progress feels slow or obstacles seem insurmountable. Building staying power starts with self-awareness. You need to understand your strengths and weaknesses, your motivations, and the factors that drive you. It also requires self-management—developing the habits and routines that keep you grounded and focused, even when the going gets tough. By regularly revisiting your intentions, you create a roadmap that guides your decisions and keeps you focused on the long-term game.

Summary of Practice 2: Activate with Intention

Through the concept of the "middle voice," we begin to take ownership in knowing that we're both the architect of our actions and the beneficiaries of their outcomes. By aligning our daily actions with our desired feelings, we can begin to experience growth that's not only external, but deeply personal.

By Activating Intentions, the path to success becomes more about who we're becoming rather than simply what we're achieving. This practice encourages ongoing reflection, personal growth, and alignment with our values. Through intentional living, we can cultivate a life that feels fulfilling and meaningful.

Implications for Innerwork

- Shift your focus from rigid goal setting to intention setting.
- Identify three feelings that resonate deeply with you and can serve to guide your daily actions.
- Regularly assess if your current and contemplated actions align with the key feelings you wish to cultivate for yourself.
- Share your intentions with a trusted mentor for support and accountability.

Implications for Teamship

- Create a team culture where collective intentions, rather than fixed goals, guide decisions and actions.
- Encourage open dialogue about both individual and team intentions to ensure alignment.
- Use regular check-ins to assess if the team's actions are aligned with its desired outcomes and values.
- Assign accountability partners within the team to support one another's growth and alignment and celebrate when actions and intentions are in harmony.
- Foster adaptability within the team to adjust intentions as circumstances evolve.

Practice 3

ACT PURPOSEFULLY

Surround yourself with people who support your journey, challenge your thinking and hold you accountable to your goals.

The concept of success and fulfillment has always been deeply intertwined with the relationships and connections we nurture throughout our lives. Mitch Albom wrote in *The Five People You Meet in Heaven*, "Strangers are just family you have yet to come to know. You may think this is strange, but all endings are also beginnings. We just don't know it at the time. Each affects the other, and the other affects the next, and the world is full of stories, but the stories are all one."[14]

This sentiment profoundly speaks to me, as it highlights the deep interconnectedness of our lives and the lasting impact we have on one another. Albom's words remind us that a meaningful life is not measured by individual achievements alone but by the relationships we build and the positive impact we create within those connections. It encourages me to reflect on the companions in my life—friends, family, coworkers, and life

---

[14] Mitch Albom. *The Five People You Meet in Heaven*. Hyperion, 2003.

partners—who shape my journey and provide opportunities for laughter, growth, and shared experiences. These are the people who inspire me to strive for a life of purpose and joy.

The most satisfying companions are those with whom I share, grow, and evolve. I am a sister, a child, a grandchild, a friend, a boss, a work companion, a professional networker, a social member, and one day, I will become a partner and possibly a mother. Each role carries a responsibility to foster relationships that uplift and support, while also challenging me to be my best self.

My relationships reflect my values, choices, and self-worth. They have the power to lift me up, push me to grow, and sustain me through life's highs and lows. But I've also experienced how they can hold me back, drain my energy, and keep me tethered to patterns that no longer serve me. Albom's reminder that every ending is a new beginning fills me with hope and a renewed commitment to embrace change, nurture meaningful connections, and leave a positive mark on the lives of those I encounter.

"Is this serving me?" is a question we usually ask ourselves when we're deciding if the objects or routines in our lives still bring us joy or value (props to *Tidying Up with Marie Kondo*[15] and James Clear's *Atomic Habits*). I have diligently extended this question to the impactful yet challenging sphere of my companion relationships. These include friends, family, work companions, life partners, and my broader professional and social networks. Inspired by the wisdom of the German poet Johann Wolfgang

---

[15] *Tidying Up with Marie Kondo*, directed by Jade Sandberg Wallis, written by Marie Kondo, starring Marie Kondo, released January 1, 2019, on Netflix, https://www.netflix.com/title/80209379.

von Goethe's "Tell me with whom you consort and I will tell you who you are,"[16] I began reevaluating my companionships.

I started by writing down all of the companions in my life, and, for each, the qualities that I want to embody for that person. To put those qualities into action, I wrote a mission statement for who I want to be in each companionship to create the relationship that I want. I took into account all my relationships that already exist, how they're currently showing up in my life, how I want to be better in them, and how I make sure they continue to serve me. I also wrote this for the relationships that do not yet exist but I hope to one day have. This practice is about manifesting the person I want to be in relation to the companions I have and those I wish to welcome into my life. It is not an exercise in wishful thinking aimed at changing or influencing other people's behaviors, attitudes, or actions. Instead, it focuses on taking control of my own growth to ensure I continue to be the best version of myself. By doing so, I can foster relationships that remain meaningful and prosperous while growing in alignment with the companions in my life as circumstances and events unfold.

---

[16] "Quote by Goethe (Stefan Aug. Doinas trad.): 'Tell me with whom you consort and I will tell you who you are; if I know how you spend your time, then I know what might become of you.'" Johann Wolfgang von Goethe, Goodreads, accessed on May 22, 2024, https://www.goodreads.com/quotes/6774650-tell-me-with-whom-you-consort-and-i-will-tell.

MASTERING INTENTIONS

Myself	Parents	Siblings
• Loving • Self-compassionate • Kind • Honest • Resilient • Growth-oriented • Forgiving • High Standards	• Patient • Compassionate • Reliable • Prioritize communication • Supportive	• Reliable • Best-friend • More engaged and present • Protector
Hold myself to a higher standard while still remembering to be kind and loving towards myself and actively work to silence self-doubt.	*Be more compassionate, patient and caring towards their needs while understanding we have different ways of giving and receiving love.*	*Recommit myself to becoming a reliable best friend and remember that my responsibility to protect them is not an obligation.*
Extended Family	**Friendships**	**Future Romantic Partner**
• Understanding • Present • Adaptable • Grateful	• Fun • Compassionate • Reliable • Supportive • Loyal	• Feminine • Strong, but not overpowering • Vulnerable • Open to love • Beautiful inside and out • Communicative
Cultivate relationships rooted in understanding, allowing space for our differences and embracing the evolving nature of our connection.	*As we grow in different directions, continue to celebrate the paths life takes us on.*	*Open myself to receive love and being vulnerable. I don't need to always be strong in every relationship.*
Leadership Team	**Employees**	**Clients**
• Raise the bar • Visionary • Lead by example • Empowering • Respected • Decisive • Committed • Accountable to excellence	• Strong • Courageous • Visionary • Fair • Hardworking • Collaborative • Empathetic • Solution-oriented	• Honest • Relentless • Hardworking • Innovative • Committed • Ethical • Creative
The best leaders set the highest standards and hold themselves accountable every day.	*Own my responsibility and celebrate the commitment and contribution to our growth.*	*Work with clients who want to be partners and grow in business together.*

How to Manifest Intentional Relationships

I allow my companions to participate in and cocreate my life with me using a Companion Audit framework. I do this by curating intentional practices with each category of my companions, providing expectations for how to better deal with me, and me with them. The purpose of my Companion Audit is to support my practice of manifesting intentional relationships; that's because the power of manifestation is a phenomenally strong practice in my life. I conduct this practice regularly, not only to manifest personal and professional achievements, but to manifest the relationships and the type of people I hope to attract in my life.

I started manifesting the writing of this book when I was eight years old. I would manifest the feeling of how it felt to have the words flowing out of my brain and onto the paper. The way the keyboard sounded when I would feverishly type. How proud I would feel when it was finally completed. It's easier to understand manifestation when it's a tangible "thing" you are manifesting, but how do you manifest a person? How do you manifest a relationship? A partner whose arms I would wake up in every morning and who would kiss me on the forehead before I start getting ready for the day? A colleague who would pass by my desk in the middle of the day to make me laugh and who made the office feel like a second home? A boss that would say "good job" and make me feel like my contribution is valued and that my hard work was appreciated and recognized?

What I'm about to share has been the single most productive and life-changing practice in my life. It's allowed me to redefine relationships as they change, save friendships with people I've lost touch with, and reflect on how I grow in relation to the companions in my life. I use it to inventory and be proactive with all of my relationships so I can be more intentional about how they serve me, and I them.

One of the biggest and hardest lessons I've had to learn in life is that people change. Whether we want them to or not, people often change because life changes them. When this happens, this framework reminds me of the way I want to feel about myself and these companions. Therefore, if and when life changes and the relationship changes as a result, I remind myself what I want to have, feel, and what I'm deserving of.

This practice is so fundamental to me that I have the framework hanging on a wall at my home and look at it every morning before I start my day. You can start by listing all of your life companions across four categories:

- **Family Companions:** Parents, siblings, grandparents, and children
- **Life Partner Companions:** Our spouses or significant others
- **Friend Companions:** Mutual relationships formed during our life journey
- **Work Companions:** Colleagues, team members, clients, supervisors, and employees

Family Companions

Family is one of the most significant relationships in our lives, but it's also among the most complex. This is because family bonds are often the strongest, deepest, and longest-lasting connections we have. Love, history, expectations, and obligations connect us to our families; they're with us through every phase of life, and the relationships within a family are deeply intertwined with our experiences and growth.

In the early stages of life, we're often willing to do anything for our family members, which can sometimes mean tolerating behaviors or dynamics that we might not accept from others. This sense of duty and unconditional support can be both a strength and a challenge.

Additionally, family dynamics aren't static; they evolve with life stages and societal changes. Understanding and navigating these dynamics requires self-awareness, empathy, and sometimes professional support. By recognizing the complexity of family relationships and employing effective strategies, families can foster stronger, more resilient connections and a supportive environment.

Seeing as family relationships are often the most complex and challenging to assess, the question "Is this serving me?" doesn't imply cutting ties with family members who don't fully understand or support your journey. Instead, it means setting boundaries that protect our emotional well-being and allowing ourselves to engage in a way that feels healthy and supportive. Sometimes, this might involve difficult conversations or redefining your role within the family dynamic.

Questions to Ask About Your Family Relationships:

- Does this person love me selflessly and want what's best for me? This is one of the hardest and scariest questions to ask ourselves about our family relationships because it is the emotion we crave the most.
- Am I able to honestly communicate with my family? Communication and understanding is a key element to giving and feeling love.
- Have we grown closer together or apart over time? Taking the time to reflect on how the relationship has changed over time is important to understanding human evolution and the paradigm shifts in a relationship.
- Are there external factors that impact our relationship? Oftentimes, there are factors outside of our control that impact the relationship we have with our family members, like the introduction of new significant

others and their families by extension, for example. The role money plays in the relationship and how it impacts power dynamics and controls that may exist. Illness, mental health, addiction, and abuse are also traumatizing factors that change our relationships with our families and have a tremendous personal impact when they influence our other relationships.

Parents are Human, Too

The most significant shift between childhood and adulthood is when we recognize that our parents are human, too. We start to reevaluate, reconsider, or change our perspective of their "mistakes" or traumas and acknowledge that they have their own. Growing up, children often blame themselves for their parents' "mistakes"—we see this all too often with children of divorce and in abusive families. Children carry the weight of that burden and it impacts their self-worth and self-love as they grow up. Leaving these traumas unaddressed can create long-term impact for the relationship we have with ourselves and others. For some it can create a trauma loop, where we repeat the learned trauma—or the effects of the trauma—over and over into other relationships.

For example: if a child witnesses a parent cheating on another parent, the trauma loop becomes that they witnessed cheating and have now made it acceptable in their own mind, or that they are fearful of being cheated on so they are unable to enter new relationships with trust that it won't happen to them. Conversely, if they address and cope with the trauma, they can be mindful of the event that happened and make a concerted effort to not allow history to repeat itself in their new relationships. The most important takeaway to learn through examining these relationships, experiences, and events is that parents are human and make mistakes, they have flaws and struggle with their own demons—which is not a reflection of who their children are as people and thus shouldn't change their own self-worth.

After my father was convicted, he lost the will to live. As my family faced the hardest battle, the man I always knew to be one of the strongest fighters was ready to give up. At twenty-seven, I was too scared to leave him alone, so I started sleeping on his couch because I feared he wouldn't make it through the night. The day after he was sentenced to seventy-two months in a federal state penitentiary, I almost lost him for good. I remember sitting next to him in the hospital bed. I was crying and begging for him to live while he was begging for me to let him go. I didn't understand how he could be so selfish and weak that he would just give up now; but he was so ashamed and embarrassed of what he'd done, the mistake he'd made, and the lives he'd damaged along the way. He was a well-meaning man who'd made grave errors along the way and got very lost in the process. I just kept repeating, "But what about me? I need you."

Maybe in my own right I was being selfish, too. It has taken me years to unpack the trauma of that period of my life. A man I loved, a hero in my eyes, had made a mistake, had hurt a lot of people and didn't want to live with the guilt and pain of that anymore. He was no longer invincible to me. He was just human.

How Perception Changes Sibling Reality

Naturally there are many shared experiences within the family unit. As we grow up together, we play together, celebrate milestones together, ride the school bus together, and go on vacations together. The shared experiences refer to the day-to-day activities, too, not just the big milestone moments. You can grow up in the same exact house with the same means and experiences but have dramatically different perceptions about your relationships and your upbringing which change your reality. This comes into play most often with siblings.

My siblings and I had the same exact upbringing: we were loved equally by both of our parents. When we were young, our parents got divorced. I was eight years old, my brother was six, and my sister was four. It was the same hardship that we all experienced together, but because of our ages, awareness, and emotional and mental maturity, we all had very different responses to the divorce, which has had a lifelong impact on each of us.

For me, I took on the role of the mouthpiece and protector for my siblings. At a young age, I grew up very quickly and realized that I needed to be strong for them. While this made me outwardly brave and outspoken, it also made me emotionally isolated because I wanted them to feel like everything was going to be okay. While I look back on that and realize how much that experience shaped me into the courageous and fearless entrepreneur I am now, that was not the case in my adolescent years. Unable to communicate and connect, I slowly started slipping into a depression which lasted the better part of a decade. While my response to the trauma was to become fearless and brave, my sister's was nearly the complete opposite.

While we were absolutely safe and loved in our household, she became fearful and filled with anxiety at a young age. The separation and split between households, the constant movement, and the change in environment manifested a much different response. She was a baby without any tools or understanding of the situation.

This often plays out in nearly every single situation with families, and it multiplies over time. Committing time to communicating and dissecting these experiences together becomes profoundly valuable to creating stronger familial bonds based on understanding, respect, and love.

Life Partner Companions

Our life partners are among the most significant relationships in our lives; they're foundational to our emotional well-being and overall life satisfaction. With a life partnership, it's important to consider not only what you're receiving but also what you're contributing. Does your partner support your growth and aspirations? Do they encourage you to be your best self? Are you bringing the same value to their life? Do both partners feel loved, nourished, and valued in the relationship? Choosing your significant other if you're single is one of the most important decisions that you'll make to build the life that you want. Your life partner becomes your rock—someone with whom you grow and build together—and I very strongly advocate that at the heart of that decision is communication.

I will never forget the morning when I ended my seven-year relationship, a relationship with a man who loved me unconditionally and had every intention of marrying me. I was awake for hours thinking about how I was going to find the courage and strength to end it. I was heartbroken and I hadn't even said the words, but it was so damn hard to even find them. In fact, there *were* no words—no words to make it easier. To break someone's heart when they've done absolutely nothing wrong and you still love them, you just aren't *in love* with them anymore.

The hours of conversation that followed were gut wrenching. As the tears poured down both of our faces, I kept telling myself to be strong. Convincing myself that this was the right decision, the hardest part was over, and that I couldn't go back now as I tried to shove seven years of our life into one suitcase to bring to a hotel, to leave before I would collapse. I will never forget the pain I caused that day, all knowing it was for the greater good for both of us.

He was my best friend. He was my rock. But he had also become my comfort zone and I his. We were both destined to live magical, spectacular lives filled with excitement and joy outside of that relationship. Walking away from something that was easy and safe for me to follow my heart and my dreams of becoming a person that was meant to be bigger than who I was in the relationship, well, it was a leap of faith I knew I needed to take in myself.

How would I define a strong partner? To me, a strong partner is someone who:

- Loves me unconditionally
- Holds me accountable
- Inspires me to become better
- Will defend me without question to the outside world
- Can sit in silence with me during the most painful moments in life
- Is committed to growing with me

- Doesn't always know what to say but knows that being present matters more than anything else
- Will never stop trying to make me laugh
- Understands the importance of communication, honesty, and loyalty

Friend Companions

We often choose relationships based on shared values, interests, and experiences. But as we grow and change, it's natural for some friendships to no longer align with our evolving selves. Ask yourself:

- Do my friendships still reflect who I am today?
- Do they bring me joy and support my goals?
- Are they reciprocal, or do I give more than I receive?

Friendships should be a source of joy and mutual support, not stress or obligation.

Nurturing Friendships

Friendships take investment. It's natural to grow apart and for friendships to change as we become older. The same commonalities we had with our childhood friends may be yet a distant memory. The conveniences we shared with our former roommates no longer exist. That's why it's important to continue to reevaluate and redefine the friendships that you have in your life as the manner in which they exist and the significance they have in your life will inevitably change over time.

Over the past year, this framework has allowed me to rekindle two very important friendships in my life—friendships that I had damaged because I stopped contributing to the relationship. Being able to repair these friendships required ownership, responsibility, apology, and concentrated effort. It wasn't just a matter of an acknowledgement and an apology, it required work and attention—the same effort required of anything in life that's worth maintaining.

Prior to establishing this framework, it was easy for me to discount distance between friendships by blaming it on physical distance, life circumstances, or new relationships. I'd say, "We no longer live in the same place," "We're both very busy right now," or "They're focused on their significant other now."

This framework forced me to take ownership of my failed participation in relationships, acknowledge my feelings and theirs, and then make an effort to become more present and prioritize the relationship moving forward. It became the starting block for identification and, in turn, opened a window for dialogue to begin the repair process: listening to their wants and needs, expressing mine, and acting responsibly based on how we both intend to mend the relationship.

While I've identified the friendships that are worth the time, effort, and energy to repair, there are also friendships that no longer deserve the same time, effort, and energy they once did. Thinking about and evaluating the quality of all of our friendships is integral to our growth as we mature and progress through life. The questions I use to guide my friendship reflections are:

- **Feelings:** What are some ways in which this relationship makes me feel?

- **Effort:** Does this person put in an equal effort as I do? How does it make me feel?
- **Values:** Does this friend continue to share the same values we once shared together?
- **Commonality:** Do we continue to have any commonalities between us that bring us joy and happiness?
- **Accountability:** Does this person continue to hold me accountable and support me in the journey to become a better version of myself?
- **Understanding:** Does this person make me feel understood and appreciated?
- **Jealousy:** Is jealousy becoming a more dominant theme? I find this to be the most significant factor in why relationships fracture as we get older (more on this in a bit).

In life, we will outgrow various friend circles as time progresses and goes on, and friendships will take on different meanings. That is not a reflection of ourselves, but instead that it becomes part of the natural transition of life. This topic becomes a challenging one because it starts to look and feel "transactional," but that's not the intention. The intention is to commit yourself to redefining and prioritizing your friendships as life circumstances change so you can hold the ones who are dear to you close and allow the ones that may be hurting and hindering your growth, happiness, and prosperity to transition out of your life with grace and understanding.

How do you define a good friend, one you think is worth keeping in your life? To me a good friend is someone who:

- Is there for me
- Supports me

- Is present for me during the big and small moments in life
- Brings joy to my life and makes me laugh
- Makes me feel understood
- Wishes the best for me

Jealousy in Friendships

One of the most complicated factors that begins to impact friendships as we transition and develop becomes jealousy. Especially if you're on the road to self-discovery and personal growth, friends who don't maintain that same commitment to self-awareness often experience jealousy in the relationship, which will fracture bonds and leave you feeling isolated and confused. Where I see this the most is with the introduction of significant others to the friendship; a relationship between two friends becomes impacted by a third or fourth party, someone who wasn't there for the start of the friendship and who doesn't hold the bond as closely.

To bring up jealousy when discussing friendships feels uncomfortable, but it does become a reality that needs to be addressed. It doesn't mean that the relationship can no longer exist or that it doesn't have a place in your life, but it is a component to be mindful of when redefining your commitment to that friend and how that relationship shows up in your day-to-day. If you're to become the best version of yourself, you need to know you're deserving of the strongest relationships in your life and hold yourself to the highest accord. No friend should negatively impact your self-worth and contribution to the world—if they do, that relationship is no longer serving you.

Advice on Nurturing Friendships

Friendships go two ways and require mutual and intentional effort. A friend of mine, an introvert, has a spreadsheet that she uses to be intentional in how she tracks her efforts with her closer friends. She explicitly holds herself accountable for how and when she reaches out and touches base. She pings her friends so that she doesn't take them for granted. She is intentional and proactive in nurturing her close friends, who are disproportionately more important to her *because* she's an introvert.

Work Companions

Work companions shape us in ways that we often underestimate. As we progress in our career, it's strange to recognize that our work companions ultimately become the people we spend the most time with. Oftentimes we don't explicitly choose the people we work with, yet they have a profound impact on our professional development, growth, commitment, and enthusiasm for the organization. I would argue that workplace relationships can be one of the most important factors that attribute to workplace retention and personal growth within an organization. Having friends at work can be one of the most rewarding parts of the job (I know that's how it's been for me).

Even with the stress and frustration that exists on a day-to-day basis with the product we turn out, knowing that I get to work with and around people I admire, respect, and who make the workplace fun makes a stressful environment far more enjoyable. In a way, the workplace feels like a second home and colleagues like another family. To me, that's the best way to work and was a core competency and requirement when starting and growing my company, The Masters Division. And it's worked: since 2021, we've grown to become one of the largest residential real estate marketing and sales teams in the United States, representing a $10 billion global real estate portfolio.[17] In 2023, we were ranked fourteenth in the nation, and first in New York City and New York state for transaction volume.[18]

Workplace relationships also have complexities that don't exist in the other companionship relationships. Whenever you introduce titles, politics, hierarchy, and money, relationships and motivations begin to shift and change. With those added factors, professional relationships become one of the most fluid and rapidly changing companionships within the framework. It's no surprise that the faster you accelerate and move up a corporate ladder, the quicker you'll learn the difference between who supports you and who is threatened by you. It's important to understand who is genuinely in your corner and who isn't. It's a tough pill to swallow and, unfortunately, a dynamic that can change on a dime.

How do the principles of mastering intentions play to our relationships with our coworkers? We have bosses, subordinates, and colleagues, and they're all coworkers, adults, and professionals that we see on a regular basis. I define work companions broadly as anyone I deal with in the conduct of my work, and it's not hierarchical between customers, suppliers, colleagues, staff, direct reports, or reporting levels above me. While they all have relatively different power dynamics, they're all coworkers

---

[17] https://therealdeal.com/magazine/national-april-2023/ranking-nycs-top-residential-brokers/
[18] https://www.realtrends.com/ranking/best-real-estate-agents-new-york/teams-mega-volume/

at the end of the day. When we think of a coworker, we unconsciously overlook our suppliers and our customers, but they too are people we work with.

Questions to evaluate your work companions:

- Are your work companions aligned with your professional values and goals?
- Do they challenge you in positive ways and provide opportunities for growth?
- Do they drain your energy, undermine your confidence, or create a toxic work environment?

What's important to being a good work companion?

- Do I bring joy and positive energy to the workplace?
- Do I execute my deliverables on time and with pride?
- Am I willing to learn from others?
- Am I open to teaching others?
- Do I communicate effectively?

I've tried to create a family in the workplace. I aim to accomplish this through culture, camaraderie, enthusiasm, and support when people are struggling through a difficult time. I aim to create an environment where people can fail forward and learn from their mistakes; where they won't be judged or reprimanded, but instead given an opportunity to reflect and course correct; where there's a standard of taking ownership for their mistakes and a commitment to not repeat them.

It's not lost on me that everyone has a different family that they left or dealt with before or after they walk in or out of our office doors. This is an insight that is also overlooked and under appreciated by many so-called people managers. Understanding this is the most important part to how people are motivated when they show up to the office. In other work eras, few cared what a worker did when they left the office, where they came from, or what they went home to. But to me, this is the why: understanding your peoples' people is the most important thing you can do.

When it comes to understanding the motivations of my coworkers in the context of before or after they pass through the office doors, it becomes a fine line to navigate. When we're at the office, we all still have a job to perform, so I don't want to cross the boundary between becoming too personal in a way that impacts the work product. However, I have found that the people who are most connected to my organization are the ones who talk about their family. We talk about their kids, their dog, and can share and laugh together about those experiences—as long as we set the expectation that we assure the work gets done and are in this together, both in the office and out of it. In this way, teamship becomes a function of communication, transparency, and honesty in giving someone the support that they want or need.

Understand Your People's People

Intentional practices I use to master relationships with my work companions include understanding my people's people, leading with compassion and providing financial planning resources. From day one of starting The Masters Division, I've said I hire for people, not for a position. If the person sitting across from me is the right person, I will find a position for them *every single time*.

Prior to hiring anyone, one of the most important things I want to learn about someone is their family, their people, because the presence or absence of family shapes who we are. They can become our biggest enablers, a driving force, a source of inspiration, or something that holds us back. The hardest workers I have ever met are people whose entire family depends on them to pay the bills. The best entrepreneurs I've ever met are ones who had something to prove because of the way they were treated by their family. The most resilient people are ones who had traumatic childhoods and learned resilience from a young age. Conversely, the people who burn out the fastest are the ones who never had to work for anything before. The laziest workers are the ones who grew up entitled and enabled. The employees who don't respect hierarchy, structure, or process learned this from a young age because they grew up without rules and repercussions.

While understanding your people's people is imperative, it's also important to realize that your people often can't control the people in their own lives. Raising children, managing parental relationships, and coping with marital problems take time. If someone is focused on their family at home but is forced to come into the office, they're not going to do their best work. The way you best connect with your people is by allowing them to be there for their people when they need to be. Companies that have the best practice of allowing their people to be there for their people during those times of need have the most buy-in from their employees. If you can lead with compassion, empathy, and understanding, your employees will be more aligned with your brand, your vision, and with you as a leader.

Understanding your people's family dynamics, financial pressures, family planning goals, and career aspirations will allow you to work one-on-one with your employees to develop a career roadmap that best suits their aspirations. Personally, I aim to create a pathway for success for my people so that they can feel tangibly supported to achieve what they're trying to do with their family units. In this way, they feel their work and contribution is valued and this translates back to their family goals.

Exercise 3.1: Companion Audit

A core competency in life is to be adept at managing our various companion groups of family, friends, coworkers, and partners. These companion stakeholders all have the ability to shape or derail our intentions. Therefore, the more proactive and intentional you are about managing these different relationships, the more mastery of yourself you will achieve.

Each category of companion has different expectations, needs, and practices. So how can you navigate these various stakeholders in a way that converges toward supporting your intentions?

Now that you have identified your companions, now ask yourself:

1) **How does this companion make me feel?** It's important to first evaluate the current status of the relationship.
2) **Do I see this companion as my equal?** Do you operate on an equal playing field with this companion, or is there a degree of separation in your relationship?

3) **Does this companion encourage or support me to be the best version of myself?** Does this person enhance your life, or are they holding you back or preventing you from growth?

For each companion, dive deeper:

1) Reflect on the relationship:
    - What do I value about this person?
    - What do I contribute to their life?
    - How are they showing up in my life?
2) Evaluate how the relationship makes you feel:
    - Does it energize or drain me?
    - Is it reciprocal, or do I find myself giving more than I receive?
3) Decide how you want to move forward with each of your key companions:
    - Do I want to invest more in the relationship?
    - Should I set new boundaries?
    - Should I quit this companion?
4) Write down the key qualities you wish to have between you and each specific companion.
5) Communicate with your companion.
    - Exchange feelings and needs.
6) Take actions that align with your values and well-being.
    - Quit or reduce commitment to the relationship?
    - Maintain the relationship?
    - Invest more in the relationship?

Ultimately, it's important to embrace the power of asking "Is this serving me?" in our relationships. It's a question that requires courage, honesty, and self-awareness. By applying it to our connections with companions, we create a life filled with relationships that truly serve us—relationships that support our growth, align with our values, and bring us joy.

Companions as a Mirror of Ourselves

Not all challenges in a relationship are negative. Some of the most growth-oriented relationships are those that push us to confront uncomfortable truths about ourselves and help us evolve. The key is distinguishing between a relationship that is nurturing and one that is depleting.

Remember, you don't have to do it alone. Relationships play a crucial role in sustaining our staying power. Surround yourself with people who support your journey, challenge your thinking, and hold you accountable to your goals. Good friends, mentors, and colleagues can provide the encouragement and perspective you need when the road gets tough. They can remind you of your strengths when the Brain Bully gets loud, and they can help you stay focused on the bigger picture when you're tempted by short-term gains.

As Vincent van Gogh wisely said, "Close friends are truly life's treasures. Sometimes they know us better than we know ourselves. With gentle honesty, they are there to guide and support us, to share our laughter and our tears. Their presence reminds us that we are never really alone."[19]

---

[19] "Quote by Vincent van Gogh: 'Close friends are truly life's treasures. Sometimes they know us better than we know ourselves. With gentle honesty, they are there to guide and support us, to share our laughter and our tears. Their presence reminds us that we are never really alone.'" Vincent van Gogh, Goodreads, accessed July 28, 2024, https://www.goodreads.com/quotes/463648-close-friends-are-truly-life-s-treasures-sometimes-they-know-us.

Summary of Practice 3: Act Purposefully

We can't underestimate the importance of surrounding ourselves with the right companions—those who support our growth, challenge our thinking, and hold us accountable. Meaningful relationships shape our lives and nurturing them requires intentionality. By conducting the Companion Audit, you'll be able to dive deeper into the companionships that currently exist and shape your life. Ultimately, the practice of evaluating and intentionally nurturing relationships leads to a life filled with meaningful connections that contribute to your growth, happiness, and success.

Implications for Innerwork

- Conduct a Companion Audit to evaluate the relationships in your life.
- Ask yourself, "Is this serving me?" and adjust your relationships accordingly.
- Intentionally nurture the relationships that uplift you, challenge your thinking, and hold you accountable.
- Be open to releasing those relationships that no longer serve your higher purpose.
- Be aware that not all relationship challenges are negative, some push us to grow and evolve.

Implications for Teamship

- Facilitate team discussions that encourage members to evaluate their personal and professional relationships in alignment with their purpose.

- Ensure that team roles and dynamics support individual growth while contributing to the team's collective purpose.
- Establish clear boundaries and expectations within the team, ensuring that everyone's emotional well-being is considered.
- Gather to celebrate and/or express gratitude.

INTENTION TWO

Amplify Your Power

Practice 4

HARNESS YOUR INNER CONFIDENCE

Our brain is the most powerful force in the world.

A few years ago, I was in one of the properties I was representing as a real estate broker, shooting photos to prepare the home to come on the market. As I told the photographer, "Stand there, move the camera up six inches, pull out the frame, and shoot it from this vantage point."

"See this," as I signaled with my arms opened, extending them away from my body into a V formation, "this is what I want to capture right here."

He turned to me and said something I have never forgotten: "One of the most incredible things about you is not your confidence, but your decisiveness. You make a decision, and you stick with it. It doesn't matter what you say next because you say it with so much conviction, I am going to believe you."

The biggest misconception about confidence is most believe that people are born with it. Let me set the record straight: confidence is a *learned skill set* that compounds over time. No one is just born confident. Some learn it earlier than others because their childhood exposes them to experiences that allow them to exhibit confidence during life's most transformative years, but no one is confident without practicing *how to become* confident.

In that moment, I knew I was a confident person because I had worked so hard to become one; what I hadn't realized was that my decisiveness was the root of my confidence. Lessons that were taught to me at a young age gave me the foundation to build my confidence as a child. When I think back to my mom telling me at a clothing store, "Walk up to the saleswoman and ask her if she has your size," I realized that she was teaching me to be aware of my body language and to speak with authority and conviction. "Come to a consensus, pick up the phone, and order," was my dad teaching me to be diplomatic and decisive when it came to ordering takeout for my family. When I started thinking about how subtly my parents taught me these lessons, I started changing how I framed teaching and sharing confidence, because it boils down to the most basic thing: your voice.

Own Your Voice, Decide, And Stick to It

Most executives lead very successful careers, getting their decisions right—most of the time. They pay extra attention to what they consider consequential decisions and generally delegate the reversible decisions.

Consequential decisions are those that will have long-term impacts on your life and business. They are difficult to reverse, require substantial analysis, extensive consultation with others, and alignment with your core values. Executives approach these decisions cautiously as they can significantly impact their futures. In contrast, reversible decisions have short-term impact, carry lower stakes, and are easily changed. Those decisions can be made quickly. Understanding the distinctions helps me prioritize my focus.

Invest your time and resources in evaluating the consequential decisions in your life. To avoid getting bogged down in unnecessary deliberation, decide quickly on the reversible ones to enable you to keep moving forward. Own it and make decisions. That is how you start to build confidence.

Exercise 4.1: Always Make the Ask

I remember when my family would go out to dinner as a child. As I read the menu and tried to pick what I would eat, the waiter approached me, gestured the pen in his hand, and said, "And for the young lady?"

I looked up at my mom, pointed to the menu, and whispered, "Can I get this?"

She responded, "Sit up straight and tell the man what you want."

This was an early lesson in the power of articulating my wants to others, a premise that was clarified years later during a study abroad trip to China.

While there, a Babson College professor, Kevin Mulcahy, completely shifted my thinking about "asks." During a class, he imparted one of the best and most memorable pieces of advice I've ever received: to "always make the ask." He assured the class that we would never get hurt by asking for something. He said there are only three answers "Yes, no, or no response at all." He challenged us to start "counting our asks" and gave us a framework to follow.

1) Start by setting a goal (such as, I will make five "asks" this week).
2) Develop a plan: list all the people you are meeting with this week.
3) Identify your want: write down what you would like to achieve from the meeting and identify the end goal.
4) Make the "ask": what is the question you need to ask that person to move toward your goal?

He then instructed me to keep making "asks" until I got to a no. With every yes, you start to build more confidence. With every question that never got a response, I would learn to pivot and redirect. I would find another question and ask that instead. If no is the worst thing that I could hear, then what happened when I would hear it? Would my confidence be shattered? I realized that if I wasn't getting to no, then my "asks" were not big enough because absolutely nothing happens when someone tells you no. But the fear of the no is what keeps us from asking.

In the same way that the fear of making decisions keeps us indecisive, indecision fuels anxiety. Anxiety is a feeling of fear, dread, and uneasiness.[20] Developing decisive practices and behaviors is fundamental to building confidence, resilience, and amplifying our power. But why are so many people indecisive? Why is it so hard to make that decision and stick to it?

---

[20] Merriam-Webster, s.v. "anxiety," accessed August 2, 2025, https://www.merriam-webster.com/dictionary/anxiety.

The Brain Bully is the Enemy of Our Intentions

Our minds are powerful. At our best, we're each capable of extraordinary creativity, reasoning, emotion, and problem-solving. However, we also host an unwelcome saboteur of our best intentions. This saboteur is known as the Brain Bully, a concept I was introduced to by my media coach, Lynn Smith, when I began working with her a few years ago. While I learned so much from her, one of the most valuable practices I took away from our sessions was how to let go of the preconceived notions I was harboring in my mind to show up as my strongest and best self. Although she was preparing me for formal media and live television appearances, this practice has also proven invaluable in my everyday life.

The Brain Bully is an inner critic, generating negative and discouraging thoughts that often make us feel sad, worried, or inadequate. You experience it as that inner voice that tells you that you're not good enough, that you're going to fail, or that others are better than you.

The Brain Bully is particularly toxic when we set intentions for ourselves. When we aspire to achieve something, this inner voice rears its ugly head, amplifying our self-doubt, constricting our confidence, and subverting our intentional mindset. It acts to generate obstacles between us and our intentions. The obstacles come forth as negative thoughts to provoke and distort reality. These bullying thoughts are not truths; they are not based on facts or evidence. They are instead products of our innate fears and insecurities. While they may feel real and powerful, they can be challenged and changed by mastering the powerful practice of positive self-talk.

The Brain Bully often triggers fears that can paralyze us, keeping us in a cycle of worry and inaction. This fear can cloud your judgment, preventing you from drawing on your experiences and skills. Positive self-talk helps us overcome this fear by reminding us of our capabilities and strengths, enabling us to approach challenges as problem solvers rather than succumbing to defeat.

When we radiate positivity into the universe and to the people around us, we attract positive forces in return. Our mindset shifts, allowing us to see challenges as opportunities for growth rather than insurmountable obstacles. This shift in perspective is crucial in overcoming the Brain Bully and maintaining momentum toward our goals.

The negative statements of the Brain Bully often take a form that I believe most would recognize from their own inner voices:

> *"You're not smart enough to do this."*
> *"You're not attractive enough to be loved."*
> *"You'll never be successful."*
> *"You're not talented enough."*
> *"You don't deserve happiness."*
> *"You'll never overcome this challenge."*

Overcome the Brain Bully with Self-Talk Affirmations

Even as a confident person, sometimes our confidence is shaken, and our Brain Bully creeps back in. This happens quite often, which is why the practice of positive self-talk has become a constant, daily exercise and practice in my life.

In my midtwenties, when my father was arrested, it was one of the darkest times in my life. I was utterly terrified and felt like I had no control over the outcome. I felt powerless, overwhelmed, and defeated. When I needed more strength than ever to survive and be strong for my family, getting out of bed felt nearly impossible. Every morning, I would wake up and my new reality would smack me in the face all over again. That was my life. Finding the strength to walk to the bathroom and start getting ready for the day, I would look in the mirror at myself and cry. I would say to myself:

> "I am a survivor."
> "I am strong."
> "I can do this."
> "My family needs me."
> "One day at a time."
> "It will be okay."
> "I will be okay."

None of these statements felt true at that moment, but I just kept repeating them to myself—out loud and in the mirror—daily. Day after day, I would do the same thing. In time, I stopped crying. Eventually, I started saying these affirmations a little bit louder. Months later, midway down the list, I smiled a little, feeling that, yes, I could get through this. As time passed, I started feeling a little bit stronger. And now years later, I know every single one of these affirmations to be true.

While I practice these affirmations every day, this practice helped me out of an uncomfortable situation quite recently (as of the time of writing this book).

I was sitting in my office late one summer Saturday evening. It was a lovely, brisk evening, so I opened the window to enjoy the breeze. Laser-focused on my computer screen, something flew through the window into my office. In sheer disbelief, I looked up and saw that a sizable cockroach had flown past me at lightning speed, crashing into the wall above my computer. It was at this very moment that I discovered my previously unknown, irrational fear of cockroaches.

I jumped from my desk, screamed, and stumbled out of the room. Panic swept through my body and I ran as far away as I could. It kept flapping around and ricocheting from wall to wall, and the more I watched its fury, the more anxiety arose in my body. I got hot, my face went pale, and my heart was beating out of my chest. I was frozen in place and powerless. How could something so small make me feel so scared? Looking back, it feels silly that something so small impacted me so much, but it did. I felt my nervous system crippling, my shoulders tensing, and my back hurting, and I was at a complete loss for what to do next. I needed to finish what I was working on, but how could I go back into my office? What should I do? I initiated positive self-talk to muster my resolve.

"I am strong."
"It's just a bug."
"It can't hurt me."
"I will be okay."
"It's going to be okay."

I repeated it over and over again, but I didn't believe it. Over the course of the next two hours, I continued to scream and tense up as I watched the bug fly around my office, all the time repeating my affirmations out loud. Finally, it left my office, and I ran back inside, packed my things, and fled. I was so nauseous that it took me twenty-five minutes to walk the five blocks home. I just kept repeating the same thing, out loud, adding in:

> *"Tomorrow will be a better day."*
> *"I can do this."*
> *"I will do this."*
> *"I will face my fears."*
> *"I am okay."*

I had caused damage to my body that took a few days to unravel. The cockroach that put me in the ultimate flight or fight mode taught me more lessons than I ever expected I would get from a bug.

When I woke up the next day, completely derailed from the intentions I had set out the night before, I was terrified to return to the office again. I pushed myself anyway, knowing that there will always be things in life that come up and try to pull us away from our intentions, but I wasn't going to let my Brain Bully control me.

> *"I am strong."*
> *"I show up."*
> *"I work hard."*
> *"I face my fears head-on."*

And that's exactly what I did.

Big or small, my positive self-talk practice is about training my mental muscle to stand up to my Brain Bully, challenge its narratives, and replace them with affirmations grounded in self-compassion and truth. Positive self-talk isn't about internally "yelling" to drown out the negativity with forced positivity, it's the practice of cultivating supportive internal dialogue to counter your Brain Bully. It involves recognizing the negative statements your Brain Bully throws at you and replacing them with positive, intentional, and abundant affirmations.

These positive statements affirm your worth and potential, reinforcing the idea that you're strong enough to overcome *and* deserving of greatness. The journey to abundant positivity begins with simple affirmations that I incorporate into my daily routine, and you can, too. Here are some good ones to start with:

> "I am strong."
> "I am deserving."
> "I am loved."
> "I am valued."

In my practice of positive self-talk, I start every morning with my affirmations. I know that my Brain Bully will challenge these affirmations at some point during the day, which is why getting my head into the right headspace before I even enter the world and see people is crucial to my morning routine and how I set myself up for success throughout the day.

My affirmations are deeply personal to me because they're a direct response to my Brain Bully, which means your affirmations will probably be different because they need to be a response to your own Brain Bully.

To overcome your Brain Bully, you must first identify the negative narrative in your mind, then create a positive self-talk affirmation that will reduce its power. For each affirmation, I've also included why that affirmation works for me. Understanding my "whys" should help you be more intentional with your own affirmations.

To ensure the robustness of my own positive self-talk affirmations, I go further and try to list three solid reasons why that positive affirmation works for me. Doing this extra step shores my belief in my affirmation—beyond self-soothing—with a phrase that might sound great but has no personal meaning. Taking the extra step to craft three "whys" for each affirmation deepens its impact.

My Brain Bully's Default Narrative	My Self-Talk Affirmation	Why This Affirmation Works For Me (My Three Ways)
"I'm not smart enough to do this."	"I'm capable of acquiring the knowledge and skills I need." "My wisdom grows with my effort."	Underlines the fact that my intelligence is not a fixed trait, but something that can be developed through dedication. Reinforces that my learning is a continuous process, and that effort is a key ingredient to wisdom and success. **By focusing on growth, I empower myself to act rather than be paralyzed by self-doubt.**
"I am not attractive enough to be loved."	"I value my true self." "I use my authenticity to forge genuine connections."	Emphasizes my inner qualities, highlights my inner character and kindness. Challenges the need for external validation for 'I am attractive.' and encourages me to value myself for who I am. **By working on my self-acceptance, I attract people who appreciate me for who I am and foster deeper and more meaningful connections.**
"I will never be successful."	"I measure my success by my own personal growth." "I enrich my life with every step I take."	Redefines success as a personal and internal journey rather than external achievements. Emphasizes the importance of my personal growth, fulfillment, and the wisdom I gain through my experiences. **By focusing on the process rather than the outcome, I cultivate personal satisfaction with my own efforts.**

"I am not talented enough."	"I am committed to honing my unique abilities." "I expand my talents through my own persistence and passion."	Underscores that talent isn't an innate gift, but something that I can develop through dedication and effort. This means I take a proactive approach to my personal development, asserting ownership over my abilities. **By focusing on growth, I strengthen my belief in my capacity to achieve my own greatness.**
"I do not deserve happiness."	"I invite joy and happiness into my heart every day." "I embrace an attitude of gratitude."	Affirms that happiness is a fundamental human right and can be cultivated through an "attitude of gratitude". Creates a mindset that attracts joy and contentment by regularly focusing on the positives in my life and appreciating what I have. **By combating feelings of unworthiness, I promote my sense of inner peace.**
"I will not overcome this challenge."	"My challenges forge my wisdom and strength." "I will emerge stronger and wiser, as I have done before."	Highlights the fact that challenges are an integral part of personal growth. Reinforces that by tackling my inevitable difficulties with an attitude of determination and resilience, I know that overcoming them will lead to my personal development. **By viewing obstacles as opportunities to gain wisdom and strength, I constantly shift to an "intentional mindset of empowerment" and avoid my "Brain Bully mindset of defeat."**

Repeating selected affirmations daily helps me rewire my brain, diverting any nascent negative self-talk with positive beliefs about myself. Over time, these affirmations have become ingrained in my subconscious, empowering me to face life's challenges with greater confidence and resilience.

Reclaim Positivity

Escaping our Brain Bully is a journey that requires self-awareness, persistence, and a commitment to nurturing a positive mindset. By practicing positive self-talk and incorporating abundance affirmations into our daily routine, we gradually weaken the influence of our Brain Bully and reclaim control over our thoughts and emotions.

We aren't our insecurities. Our Brain Bully doesn't define us. We have the power to challenge and change the narrative in our minds. With time, patience, and consistent practice, we will silence the negativity and empower ourselves to live a life aligned with our intentions and aspirations. Start today: stand up to your Brain Bully and speak to yourself with the kindness, respect, and encouragement you deserve. Our journey to evading our Brain Bully begins with one positive thought at a time.

Commit yourself to this practice daily for thirty days straight. As soon as you wake up, look at yourself in the mirror and speak out loud. If you make this a morning practice, over time you will see how this exercise becomes applicable throughout your day. You'll naturally start speaking positive affirmations to yourself, which will recalibrate your mindset and bring more positivity into your life.

Exercise 4.2: Positive Self-Talk Affirmations

This exercise aims to help you learn and practice positive self-talk, counter your negative Brain Bully, and build a more empowering and supportive practice of positive self-talk. Take these three steps to start counteracting negative thinking patterns.

1) **Identify Your Brain Bully:** Take ten minutes to reflect on the Brain Bully concept, that inner voice criticizing, doubting, and diminishing you. Using the chart below,

write down three common statements or thoughts that your Brain Bully often tells you. These might include phrases like:

"I'm not attractive enough to be loved."
"I'm not smart enough to do this."
"I don't deserve happiness."

Next to each Brain Bully statement, write a rational response that challenges the negativity. For example, if my Brain Bully says, "I'm not good enough," my response could be, "I have accomplished many things and have grown as a result."

2) **Craft Positive Affirmations:** Transform each rational response into a positive affirmation phrased in the present tense.

> *"I accomplish many things and am constantly growing."*

3) **Document Three Whys for Each Affirmation:** Write down three reasons why this positive affirmation works for you. Experiment with documenting a general statement, a belief, and a conclusion until the words resonate, tapping into your authentic, positive inner voice. This will be hard to do at first, but it does get easier with practice.

MASTERING INTENTIONS

My Brain Bully's Default Narrative	My Self-Talk Affirmation	Why This Affirmation Works For Me (My Three Ways)

Once you've created your affirmations, you must voice them. Write down your three affirmations and commit them to memory. Repeat these aloud to yourself in the mirror every day when you wake up. I say mine three times over, with more power in my voice, heart, and brain as I go.

After thirty days, reflect on your progress and ask yourself:

- How has my mindset shifted?
- Have I noticed a decrease in negative self-talk?
- Am I feeling more empowered and confident?

Like any practice, it will feel unnatural and uncomfortable as you begin, and you will need to continue refining it. But the more you engage in this exercise, the more natural it will become. Continue to update your positive self-talk as you detect other phrases your Brain Bully uses.

Over time, by doing this exercise you will:

- **Boost Self-Confidence:** Regularly practicing positive self-talk helps build and reinforce a strong sense of self-confidence. By affirming your abilities and focusing on your strengths, you can cultivate a more positive self-image and a greater belief in your capacity to achieve your goals. This increased self-confidence can improve your performance in various areas of life, from work to personal projects.
- **Enhance Emotional Resilience:** Positive self-talk will improve your ability to cope with challenges and setbacks. By framing situations more optimistically and constructively, you can reduce feelings of anxiety and self-doubt. This enhanced resilience allows you to recover more quickly from difficulties, maintain a positive outlook, and approach challenges with a problem-solving mindset.
- **Promote Overall Well-Being and Mental Health:** Positive self-talk contributes to a more positive mental state and emotional well-being. This reduces stress, increases happiness, and promotes a more proactive attitude toward self-care and personal development.

Exercise 4.3: Team Self-Talk

Positive self-talk within your corporate culture can shift the entire energy of an organization and the people within it. I encourage my teams within my organization to do this regularly throughout the day. In fact, it has become a practice we do collectively. Before going into a big meeting or a pitch, we repeat a shared affirmation to center us as a team for the meeting ahead. We say out loud:

> *"We're great at what we do."*
> *"We know our value and the level of service we provide."*
> *"We'll win this business."*

While the Brain Bully is very personal to each individual in your organization, you can create positive affirmations that apply to the culture to push your people and their intentions forward and enhance productivity and confidence within your teams.

To best implement team self-talk within your organization, conduct this exercise within small groups that work directly together on joint initiatives. Start by asking:

- How do we feel we are performing as a group?
- What do we feel is holding us back from performing better?

1) **Brainstorm** a list of all the affirmations the group feels empowered by. Read the affirmations out loud and ask:
    - Does this affirmation empower us, motivate us, and enhance our confidence?
    - If we spoke this affirmation together before every meeting, would this positively impact our mindset?
2) **Select** the top three that resonate most with the team.
3) **Verbalize** these affirmations out loud before any big team meeting, event, performance, or presentation for the next thirty days.

4) **Review** after thirty days. Convene with the team and ask team members to answer these questions individually:
   - Have I enjoyed saying these affirmations out loud?
   - By voicing these affirmations, have I felt more confident going into meetings, presentations, and so on?
   - By saying these affirmations as a group, have I felt more connected to my peers and have we performed as a stronger and more unified team?
   - Over the past thirty days, have I won more business or been more successful in my delivery during presentations/meetings?

By following this structured approach, you can effectively measure the impact of affirmations on your team's performance and cohesion. Furthermore, this exercise will create a culture of positive self-talk and collective affirmation to unite your team. The outcomes will be felt as:

- **Enhanced Morale and Motivation:** Positive self-talk can significantly boost employees' confidence and overall morale. By fostering a culture where self-affirmation and constructive self-talk are encouraged, employees are more likely to approach challenges with a positive attitude, feel more engaged, and maintain higher motivation levels. This can lead to increased job satisfaction and a more enthusiastic workforce.
- **Improved Resilience and Stress Management:** A culture that supports positive self-talk helps employees manage stress and bounce back from setbacks more effectively. When individuals are trained to use positive

self-talk, they are better equipped to handle difficult situations, reduce self-doubt, and maintain a resilient mindset. This can improve their ability to cope with the pressures of their roles and contribute to overall well-being.
- **More Supportive Collaboration:** Positive self-talk can extend beyond individual benefits to enhance team dynamics. Employees who practice positive self-talk are likely to communicate constructively and supportively with colleagues. This creates a collaborative environment where team members uplift each other, share encouragement, and work together more effectively. Such an environment promotes a culture of mutual respect and collaboration.

I started doing this practice with my team and agents a few years ago when we were gearing up to go in to pitch our services for one of the most iconic development buildings in New York City. If we won this project, it would have unquestionably changed the game for us. I was bringing my whole leadership team with me and I could tell they were a bit nervous leading up to the meeting. Normally I would have just given one of my pep talks, but this meeting required more—we needed confidence, unity, excitement, and enthusiasm. I needed everyone on my team to know we were deserving of our seat at the table and it was in our hands to win or lose, and the quickest way to lose the business before we even walked through the door was by thinking we didn't deserve to be there. So, I started speaking my affirmations out loud and had them all repeat after me.

> *"We deserve to be here."*
> *"We are the best at what we do."*

"We work harder than anyone in the industry."
"We have sold more projects than any of our competitors."
"We are prepared."
"We feel great about our strategy."
"We will win this project."

We repeated this day after day leading up to the meeting. We said this all again in the elevator on the way up to the meeting. Head high and shoulders back, we each walked into the room like we owned it, like the project was already ours. I remember leaving that meeting with so much pride because my team left everything they had in that room. They spoke with conviction and confidence. From that day on, we've done this prior to every meeting and every business pitch, and it works.

The Power of Consistency

The key to effective positive self-talk is consistency. Like any new habit, positive self-talk will take time and practice to become a natural part of your thinking. Initially, your Brain Bully will resist, but with persistent effort, you'll notice a shift in your mindset and feel more confident, capable, and at peace with yourself.

Positive self-talk is about choosing to focus on the constructive aspects of situations and maintaining a balanced perspective. It's not about denying reality or pretending that everything is perfect. Instead, it's about intentionally challenging negative thoughts and replacing them with positive affirmations. In this way, we break our cycle of self-criticism and build a foundation of self-compassion and confidence. It's about being kind to yourself, acknowledging your efforts, and believing in your potential. As we practice positive self-talk, we'll notice shifts in how we perceive challenges, setbacks, and our abilities.

Exercise 4.4: Strengths Spotlight

Understanding our strengths is a cornerstone of building confidence. We gain crucial self-awareness when we recognize what we're naturally good at. When we can align our efforts with our abilities, we improve our self-image, leading to more motivation. More motivation in life will lead us to more productivity and motivation in business, which allow us to become high performers within our organizations. By becoming high performers who play to our strengths, we can better monetize our skill set and the pathway to success will start to feel more attainable.

Additionally, we'll feel more engaged and persistent when working from a place of strength. This intrinsic motivation helps us overcome challenges and fuels resilience. By leveraging our strengths to optimize our performance, we can create positive feedback and a stronger sense of accomplishment.

Self-awareness of our strengths also improves problem-solving, as we are more likely to approach challenges creatively and confidently. It reduces self-doubt, supports positive self-talk, and helps us handle criticism constructively. Furthermore, it strengthens our relationships by allowing for more authentic interactions and effective leadership.

Ultimately, understanding and applying your strengths builds confidence and enhances every aspect of your personal and professional life, creating a robust foundation for sustained success. Figuring out how to leverage and capitalize on our strengths is an important exercise because it allows us to silo our talents alongside what we enjoy doing. I do this by conducting a strength spotlight in which I make three columns on a sheet of paper:

What Do I Enjoy Doing?	What Am I Good At?	What Am I Good At AND Recognized For?

The magic lies in the third box.

Personally, I'm fortunate enough to love what I do; it's why I've been able to be so successful. Now that doesn't mean I enjoy *every aspect* of my job, but overall, I love what I do. I've taken this approach in every job I've ever had—and guess what? I've loved all of them.

From my first job at twelve years old working at a concession stand, I realized I enjoyed unloading our inventory shipments and placing them on the shelves in the stockroom. This taught me that I was organized. Knowing this, I started taking on the inventory management responsibility and developed a system for more streamlined ordering.

When I was fourteen, I took on a job as a photographer's assistant and learned I enjoyed photography. I realized I loved the creativity and the idea of "setting up the shot." From this, I began taking up photography as a hobby and later used this skill when I started my travel blog. I also use this skill in my current role for how I photograph and market our properties, as well as how I capture and create content on social media.

When I was eighteen, I worked as a salesperson at a gym. I learned that I enjoyed talking to clients about their goals and helping them develop fitness plans and individualized sales packages to help them achieve their goals. This is when I realized I was good at sales.

When you find the way to combine what you enjoy doing with what you're good at and play in both arenas, you begin to build confidence in your practice—because you're good at it—and you do more of it—because you enjoy doing it. By doing this, your success will compound over time, leading to more success and more fulfillment in your life.

Exercise 4.5: Own Your Compliments

While we can identify our strengths by looking internally and doing the above analysis, we can also identify our strengths by observing and learning what other people know and believe us to be good at by paying attention and receiving compliments. A compliment expresses esteem, respect, affection, or admiration,[21] and far too often people don't own compliments when they're given. Generally, we receive compliments from our companions when someone recognizes our effort, attention, work product, skill set, or personality traits, for example. If someone is complimenting us, it means they see something in us. So why would we dismiss that? Instead, we need to own our compliments and learn from the compliments we're given.

---

[21] *Merriam-Webster*, s.v. "compliment (*n.*)," accessed August 3, 2024, https://www.merriam-webster.com/dictionary/compliment.

Complimenting others is a great way to spread infectious positivity. The next time you recognize quality work, contribution, effort, improvement, or progress, give some recognition—even if you're not used to giving compliments, be brave and go for it! There are a lot of things we can compliment people on, and two simple practices significantly add to the impact of a compliment:

- Address the person by their first name and state what they did well in one sentence.
- Leave space, time, and opportunity for them to respond.

To deliver a compliment successfully, it needs to be received by the other side. We need to create space for our compliment to land with that person. Whenever you recognize something, you should acknowledge it. While any form of recognition is always appreciated, in person compliments go a lot further than over email, text, or a phone call.

Recognition focuses on *acknowledging others*. It's about taking the time to notice and appreciate the contributions of the people around you—whether it's a colleague at work, a friend who always listens, a classmate who goes the extra mile, or a family member who supports you unconditionally. Recognition is about making sure they know their efforts are seen and valued.

Why does this matter? Because everyone wants to feel appreciated. Recognition is a basic human need—it fuels our sense of worth and belonging. When you acknowledge someone, you're not just giving them a pat on the back, you're affirming their value.

There's a distinction between compliments and gratitude. A compliment is an act of selfless recognition for someone else's actions with the intent to create a positive feeling for the recipient. And that recognition can go a long way in building self-esteem and confidence in others. On the other hand, gratitude is a practice of appreciation; it's used to share a positive feeling felt by the person sharing.

Owning Our Compliments

I observe companions—my colleagues, friends, and family—self-sabotage when they're given a compliment. We're guilty of doing this far more often than we realize. Here are some examples of this in action:

> "Wow, incredible work on that presentation."
> "I was able to put it together quickly."
> "You look beautiful today."
> "This outfit? I hate how these jeans make me look."
> "Wow, that was incredibly generous of you."
> "Oh, it was nothing."

Why do we undermine our work? Our contribution? Our looks? Our kindness? Why do we minimize our contribution and effort? While the Brain Bully is one saboteur, diminishing the compliments we receive is also an act of self-sabotage.

In the same way we need to rewire our brain to combat our Brain Bully, we need to rewire it to respond to compliments with ownership and pride. Using the same examples above, let's redraft the response that keeps you feeling powerful and proud: own your credit, own your value, and own the praise.

> "Wow, incredible work on that presentation."

"Thank you. The team and I worked really hard to put it together, and we're proud of how it went."

"You look beautiful today."

"Thank you, I put a lot of thought into creating this look for today."

"Wow, that was incredibly generous of you."

"I knew that they would love that, and it makes me happy to be able to do that for them."

Now think of some compliments you've received recently. Did you own them? If not, rewrite your responses. Here are some simple actions you can take to start owning your compliments:

- Recognize the compliment.
- Acknowledge the compliment.
- Reflect on the compliment.
- Give yourself permission to accept the credit offered.

Compliments highlight our strengths. Practice positive self-talk and give yourself a compliment that someone else gave to you. Remember, we should feel proud when someone recognizes our contribution, work, or effort, so don't dismiss or discredit your work. Own it!

Compliments are personal and are a gift to that person. But in a professional environment, recognition is one step above a compliment. Recognition is tied to specific achievement in an organizational environment.

Use Recognition to Spread Infectious Positivity

Research from Great Place To Work,[22] a global leader in workplace culture, describes employee recognition as "all the ways an organization shows its appreciation for employees' contributions." Great Place To Work analyzed employee survey responses from over 1.7 million employees across small, mid-sized, and large companies over several years and found that, compared to those who don't consistently feel recognized at work, people who *do feel* recognized at work are:

- "2.6x more likely to think that promotions are fair
- 2.2x more likely to drive innovation and bring new ideas forward, and
- 2.0x more likely to say people at their organization are willing to go above and beyond"

Three top-level conclusions from their research were:

1) Recognition is more meaningful when tied to specific achievements, exhibiting desired behaviors, going above and beyond expectations, and hitting milestones such as tenure.
2) The longer it takes for managers to recognize employees, the less likely employees will see the affirmations of recognition as authentic.
3) Everyone has their preference or style when it comes to giving and receiving recognition and appreciation. They suggested leveraging the principles of Gary

---

[22] Claire Hastwell, "Creating a Culture of Recognition," *Insights* (blog), Great Place To Work, March 2, 2023, https://www.greatplacetowork.com/resources/blog/creating-a-culture-of-recognition.

Chapman's book on appreciation, *The Five Love Languages*,[23] into the "Five Languages of Appreciation in the Workplace." These are:
a) *Words of Affirmation* in public or through handwritten notes.
b) *Quality Time* through giving colleagues undivided attention.
c) *Acts of Service* through asking colleagues if they want your help.
d) *Gifts* tailored to specific interests.
e) *Physical Touch* through handshakes, fist bumps, and high-fives.

Summary of Practice 4: Harness Your Inner Confidence

Building confidence is a journey that develops over time and with intentional practice. It's built piece by piece, action by action, and flourishes when we embrace challenges, learn from them, and continue to grow. Every experience is an opportunity to practice and reinforce your confidence; it's not about being born with an innate ability to be confident, it's about actively engaging with life, stepping into new roles, and believing in your capacity to handle them. Confidence, like any skill, becomes more robust and resilient through deliberate effort and a willingness to embrace growth.

---

[23] Gary Chapman, *The Five Love Languages: How to Express Heartfelt Commitment to Your Mate*, (Chicago: Northfield Publishing, 1992).

Implications for Innerwork

- Use positive self-talk to remind yourself of your capabilities and strengths.
- Silence the "Brain Bully" with affirmations that reinforce your strengths and abilities. Focus on making decisions, even imperfect ones, to boost confidence and reduce anxiety.
- Practice receiving compliments with grace and give them freely to others.
- Assure yourself that the more you engage with life's challenges, the stronger and more resilient your confidence will become.
- Cultivate the habit of "Making Asks."

Implications for Teamship

- Encourage a practice of positive self-talk as a team before important meetings or presentations to build collective confidence and bounce back from setbacks more effectively.
- Use team rituals, such as sharing affirmations, to collectively boost morale and confidence.
- Encourage team members to make requests and ask for what they need to succeed, reinforcing that asking is a desirable strength.
- Use specific and frequent recognition to celebrate accomplishments within the team.

Practice 5

ADOPT A WINNER'S MINDSET

I am but barely a fraction of the person I am meant to become.

I wish I had understood the power of vulnerability in leadership earlier in my career. This lesson didn't come quickly to me, nor did I embrace it willingly at first. But over the years, I've realized that vulnerability is not a weakness; it's a source of strength, connection, and growth. It's allowed me to lead authentically, build stronger relationships, and overcome the many challenges that have come my way.

Like I said, I didn't embrace vulnerability willingly; rather, I was forced into it when I was cast on the reality TV show *Selling the Hamptons* on MAX. I was very hesitant about saying yes to the opportunity; I was terrified to open myself and my life up and have it broadcast to the entire world, but my fear of future regret is what ultimately got me to agree. I knew I had to step outside my comfort zone if I wanted to grow, so I took the leap.

Being on the show was an entirely different ballgame. It required me to develop a new set of skills to convey my passion for real estate in an engaging and authentic way to a television audience. But the reality was that I was uncomfortable most of the time. I was used to being in control, to knowing my business inside and out. But television was a completely new experience, and I often found myself in situations where I didn't have all the answers. The experience forced me to confront my vulnerabilities head-on. I had to be open to feedback, criticism, *and* the moments when I simply didn't know what I was doing. It was humbling (to say the least) but it was also incredibly rewarding.

I thought I knew what I was signing up for, but it didn't fully hit me until about mid-season, when I realized that if I didn't get comfortable with being uncomfortable, then my story was going to be told by someone else. I remember the night we filmed the scene where I had to share what happened to my dad and how that impacted my family and my career. I could talk about real estate endlessly; I could show any property and talk to any client and negotiate the toughest of deals. But to talk about my heartbreak, trauma, and years of crippling pain for the first time to a friend, with six camera men, four audio guys, and an entire production crew watching in another room, that was a whole new level of vulnerability. At the time, I struggled to talk about what had happened to me and my family with my best friends, and now I was going to share it with a bunch of strangers—on TV—for it to be aired to the entire world.

The day after the first episode aired, the number one autofill search on Google when I searched my name was "Bianca D'Alessio's father." There was no more hiding—it was time to let go of the shame. I could either choose to own my story and share how it has changed, shaped, and strengthened me, what it has taught me, and how it has made me more compassionate and empathetic, or I could continue to allow it to be a black shadow that followed me everywhere I went, never knowing when it would pop up again and what it would destroy along the way. To be vulnerable or to be ashamed; both options were hard, but it was time to choose—and I chose vulnerability.

What I didn't realize at the time was how liberating and life-changing leading with vulnerability would become. Not only was I able to connect with the audience in a way that I never could have if I'd tried to maintain a facade of perfection, I started making stronger connections on and off camera—with my family, colleagues, clients, and nearly every companion I had in my life. I also started becoming a better friend, sister, daughter, and boss.

Being vulnerable on camera taught me that leadership isn't just about being confident and in control, it's also about being honest, human, and willing to show your true self—even when it's uncomfortable. This was a powerful lesson, one that has stayed with me in every aspect of my leadership journey.

Leadership is not a linear path and is certainly not without its struggles. But it's in those struggles—those moments of vulnerability—that we find our true power as leaders and adopt a Winner's Mindset.

A First Major Setback

I knew when I started my business that I wanted it to be built around people. I wanted to focus on growing and harvesting incredible talent and build an environment that fostered growth and inspired my people to become the best versions of themselves in business and in life. I was so excited to do something different—something I hadn't yet experienced in the real estate industry—but I underestimated how hard that would be and the responsibility that came along with it. Managing people and carrying the weight of being responsible for people's livelihoods and families was a whole new level of pressure that I never knew before. Within the first year, I lost people—and not just one: I lost about five people within a sixty-day span. It felt like the rug had been pulled out from under me.

At that time, my entire mission was centered on building a cohesive team and creating a positive, empowering culture, and I had failed. I remember questioning everything: "What am I doing wrong? Why aren't they staying? Am I cut out for this? Am I a bad leader?" It was a pivotal moment. Team morale was down and my head was so far into the operations of making things "successful" that I lost sight of what I was aiming to do in order to make it successful—which was to empower my people.

When I look back, I realize how crucial this growing pain was. I had set my expectations too high and hadn't created the proper level of support that my team needed. I was so focused on the end goal that I forgot about the journey—and the people on it with me. I realized that being a leader isn't just about setting high standards and driving toward a vision, it's also about meeting people where they are, understanding their needs, and providing the support they need to succeed.

This experience taught me the importance of vulnerability in leadership. Vulnerability is the root of connection, and connection is essential for building a culture and community. For that first year, I was moving so quickly, pretending like I had it all figured out. The reality was I didn't. I was learning one day at a time and trying to make the best decisions I could with the information I had. I thought my stoicism and confidence would create confidence within the organization. However, my "strength" adversely affected me and created an environment that didn't allow my people to come to me to ask for help—to be vulnerable with their needs—because I wasn't exhibiting any vulnerability to them.

Eventually, I was forced to confront my own shortcomings and be honest with myself about what needed to change. I had to admit that I didn't have all the answers and that I needed to be more attuned to my team's needs. To course correct, I needed to take ownership and responsibility for my actions. I brought my team together and called myself out on my miscalculation in leadership. I apologized and shared with the group that this was a learning moment for me, and hopefully for everyone else because, after all, that's why we were there, that's why we were building what we were building—so that we could learn and grow together: that was the mission, after all. When we make mistakes and take ownership for them, we can address them and then rebuild stronger, together. This was a monumental turning point for our culture.

The Power of Delegation and Building a Supportive Structure

During this time period I also learned another crucial lesson: the power of delegation and trust. I was trying to be everything for everyone and do everything without asking for help. I had told myself that was what leaders and entrepreneurs do. Boy, how wrong I was. I was the recruiter, the trainer, the problem-solver, and everything in between. Not only was this unsustainable for growth, it was disruptive to the culture and morale I was striving to build.

Delegation isn't just about offloading tasks, but empowering others to take ownership and grow in their roles. It's about trusting your team to carry out the organization's vision and mission, even when you're not there to oversee every detail. Trust is hard. My mission was to create an environment for learning, growth, and prosperity, but how could people feel comfortable to fail, learn, and grow if I was focused on control and precision?

I realized I was becoming the bottleneck of my own business. If I didn't change something quickly, the company I'd started a year earlier would quickly fail. I needed help. It was hard to admit, but it was vulnerable and it was true. While I was personally hurt by this setback, I decided to focus on the things within my control to help me better perform as a business owner and manager. By recognizing I needed help, I began building a more robust leadership structure, hiring people who could take on more responsibility and bring their expertise to the table.

That wasn't easy and there were many side steps along the way. It required me to let go of control, trust others, and accept that things might not always be done the way I would do them. By delegating more, I was able to focus on the bigger picture—on strategy, vision, and growth. More importantly, it allowed my team members to step up, take ownership, and develop their own leadership skills.

The Fundamentals of a Winner's Mindset

The most powerful leaders are those who lead with both their heads and their hearts. This lesson was cemented in my psyche during a perspective-shifting journey to the remote wilderness of Alaska.

The vastness of nature reminded me just how small people are in the grand scheme of things. Far from the hustle and bustle of New York City, I found myself completely off the grid, hours away from the nearest town. To get there, my fellow entrepreneurs and I had to take a flight to Seattle, another to Ketchikan, Alaska, then a ferry, followed by an hour-long seaplane ride, and finally, a boat ride that brought us to that breathtakingly remote destination. We were all eager to disconnect from our fast-paced lives and reconnect with what truly matters.

The remoteness, limited cell phone coverage, and hours of uninterrupted time together created the perfect environment to trigger reflection and meaningful conversations. These reflections, sparked by a group of high achieving executives from diverse industries, subsequently led me to identify three core themes essential for distilling the elements of a "Winner's Mindset" that enabled this group of high achievers to thrive both personally and professionally.

The three themes I settled on were:

1) **Maintain persistence:** Be committed to your goals with consistency and focus while being adaptable and strategic in your approach.
2) **Foster resilience:** Build the mental and emotional strength to navigate life's inevitable challenges with grace and determination. It's about understanding that setbacks aren't roadblocks, but growth opportunities.
3) **Cultivate a growth mindset:** Embrace curiosity, seek diverse perspectives, and commit to continuous learning. This mindset allows you to see challenges as

opportunities to expand your capabilities rather than as threats to your self-worth.

For each theme, I've crafted specific behaviors that, when consistently applied, will help anyone develop a winning mindset. I've included the quotes that have most inspired my leadership journey and have helped me become a better version of myself.

Each of these themes is interwoven, creating a foundation for success that is both sustainable and fulfilling. They remind me that while our time on this earth is finite, our capacity to make a meaningful impact is limitless.

Theme 1: Maintain Persistence

> *"Success is not final, failure is not fatal: it is the courage to continue that counts."*
> —Winston Churchill[24]

This quote captures the essence of disciplined persistence—the understanding that success is a journey, not a destination. It's about staying consistent, celebrating small wins, and demonstrating patience as you work towards your goals.

During college, I started my first business, a product-based marketing company that focused on business-to-business sales. It was during this time I realized I had a gap in my sales experience and training. Even though I had a sales job selling gym memberships when I was younger, I didn't possess the "go-getter"

---

[24] "Quote by Winston Churchill: 'Success is not final, failure is not fatal: it is the courage to continue that counts.'" Winston Churchill, Goodreads, accessed on August 6, 2024, https://www.goodreads.com/quotes/3270-success-is-not-final-failure-is-not-fatal-it-is.

sales skills that my peers had. I was uncomfortable on the phone and lacked confidence to "make the ask" and close deals. To get more exposure and experience, I took on an unpaid internship at Lionbridge Technologies selling translation and interpretation services to large companies. It was here that I was trained on cold calling.

It wasn't until this internship that I realized the average salesperson yields two closed transactions for every one hundred calls. I asked myself, "What did I just sign up for?"

Since I wasn't the average salesperson and had no cold calling experience, my boss told me my goal was to set up five meetings out of the five hundred calls I had to make per day—one meeting per one hundred calls. I would then hand the meeting over to him, meaning I could lean on his experience and expertise—and his conversion rate. Knowing he could close 80 percent of the clients put in front of him, that would result in four sales per week: five hundred calls to get four sales meant a 0.8 percent conversion rate. For him, if I worked two days a week making one thousand calls, setting up ten meetings and closing eight new deals a week, that was great! Why? To most that sounds terrible, but for him it was a numbers game. So I learned how to play it, too.

I pounded the phone. Every day I was there, dialing, no answer; dialing, getting hung up on; dialing to get someone on the phone and them telling me to remove them from their list; dialing, getting someone on the phone, stumbling over my words and losing the one warm body I finally was able to get a hold of. It took me six weeks—six thousand calls—before I set up my first appointment. I remember feeling exhausted; I hated cold calling. I was sitting in a room all day with Salesforce pulled up on the computer, working down a list of names, and logging each call "no answer," "hung up," or "call back in a week," but I kept going.

At the end of my internship, two of the leads converted into sales. I don't know the number of calls I made, but if I had to guess, my conversion rate was probably somewhere less than 0.00001 percent. My contribution felt insignificant and I ended that internship feeling like I'd learned and done absolutely nothing. I don't think I'd ever felt so useless in a job.

It wasn't until five years later when I started my real estate career that I realized how insurmountably valuable that position was, because now it was time to start doing it all over again. Except this time, I was cold calling to try to get people to list their apartments with me. This was disciplined persistence: showing up every single day and putting in the work, knowing that there would be thousands of moments of rejection and I would want to give up far more often than I wanted to keep going, but doing it anyway.

Three ways to Maintain Persistence are:

Embrace the Grind

> *"All overnight success takes about 10 years."*
> —Jeff Bezos[25]

Success doesn't come overnight. It requires consistent effort, dedication, and hard work. As any professional athlete will tell you, it demands long hours, repetitive drills, and a commitment to a seemingly endless journey. Trust the process, knowing

---

[25] Jeff Bezos, "Jeff Bezos At The Economic Club of Washington (9/13/18)," moderated by David Rubenstein, livestreamed on September 13, 2018, by CNBC, YouTube, https://www.youtube.com/watch?v=xv_vkA0jsyo.

that perseverance will eventually lead to success. Even when it feels insignificant, every small step forward is progress toward your goal.

Behaviors to Embrace the Grind include:

- **Commit to consistency:** Dedicate yourself to showing up daily and understanding that small, repeated actions lead to significant results over time.
- **Value feedback:** Feedback is friend, not foe. Never stop learning and never stop evolving; embrace feedback with gratitude.
- **Demonstrate patience:** The system works. You must work it out, no matter how frustrated you are or whether you feel like you have no results. Maintain a steady pace and trust the process, knowing that success often comes from prolonged effort and perseverance. Never give up; your luck can change at any time. Your success is directly related to your willingness to work and your intent to achieve it.

Catch and Release

"The art of knowing is knowing what to ignore."
—Rumi[26]

Not every opportunity or relationship is meant to be pursued. Recognize when something or someone isn't worth your

---

[26] "Quote by Rumi: 'The art of knowing is knowing what to ignore.'" Jalal ad-Din Muhammad ar-Rumi, Goodreads, accessed August 6, 2024, https://www.goodreads.com/quotes/915736-the-art-of-knowing-is-knowing-what-to-ignore.

time and energy anymore. Sometimes you must be willing to move on. Learn to let go of what's not beneficial in order to make room for what truly matters. This ability to distinguish and move on is crucial for focusing on your goals and overall well-being.

Behaviors to Catch and Release include:

- **Evaluate priorities:** Regularly assess which tasks, relationships, and opportunities are worth your time and energy.
- **Let go strategically:** Be willing to release what's not working to make room for better opportunities.
- **Focus on the essential:** Concentrate on what truly matters and adds value to your goals.

Accept Nature's Timing

> *"Adopt the pace of nature: her secret is patience."*
> —Ralph Waldo Emerson[27]

Timing can be unpredictable and out of your control. Even with perfect preparation and the right circumstances, things will sometimes go differently than planned. Accept this unpredictability and remain patient. Trust that opportunities will present themselves at the right moment and stay ready to seize them when they do.

Behaviors to Accept Nature's Timing include:

---

[27] "Quote by Ralph Waldo Emerson: 'Adopt the pace of nature: her secret is patience.'" Ralph Waldo Emerson, Goodreads, accessed August 6, 2024, https://www.goodreads.com/quotes/20326-adopt-the-pace-of-nature-her-secret-is-patience.

- **Share transparently:** Communicate openly about the timing of goals and processes to foster trust and commitment.
- **Adapt plans:** Be flexible and ready to adjust your plans when the timing doesn't align as expected.
- **Stay prepared:** Always be ready to seize opportunities when they arise, even if they come unexpectedly.

Theme 2: Foster Resilience

> *"When we are no longer able to change a situation, we are challenged to change ourselves."*
> —Viktor Frankl[28]

The expression "nevertheless, she persisted" gained significant traction after Senator Elizabeth Warren was instructed to stop speaking by Senate Majority Leader Mitch McConnell during Senator Jeff Sessions's confirmation hearing for US Attorney General on February 7, 2017. The phrase quickly went viral, symbolizing women's resilience in breaking barriers and achieving goals, even when their voices were dismissed or ignored. The phrase "nevertheless, she persisted" serves as a rallying cry, reminding everyone that persistence is crucial in the quest for respect and recognition.

Resilience is our greatest ally as we navigate the complexities of our careers and personal lives. It enables us to stay the course, to persevere when others might falter, and to emerge

---

[28] "Quote by Viktor E. Frankl: 'When we are no longer able to change a situation, we are challenged to change ourselves.'" Viktor E. Frankl, Goodreads, accessed August 6, 2024, https://www.goodreads.com/quotes/52939-when-we-are-no-longer-able-to-change-a-situation.

stronger, wiser, and more capable with each experience. As we move forward, remember to embrace the challenges that come our way. Let them shape us, teach us, and build our resilience. In doing so, we'll find that we're not just surviving the journey—we're thriving in it.

It took me quite a bit of time for my career in real estate to pick up steam. As my confidence began to build, I began to close more deals. I moved through one deal at a time, focusing on all of the elements of the transaction and delivering exceptional client service. Throughout my career, I've always recognized my perceived weaknesses and made a conscientious effort to offset them by delivering another value proposition. At this point in time, while I was lacking in experience, I knew I could differentiate by going above and beyond with my clients. I made myself available all the time, implemented my own five-minute response time to emails, always conducted my own research, and followed up with answers to questions even when I didn't know how to. I forced myself to be at the top of my game when interacting with clients because I didn't have experience to fall back on.

One day, my boss pointed out that I was spending just as much time and effort on a rental transaction as on a sale—and the latter could make me tenfold the amount of money. He told me to shift my focus and start to level up, so I started pivoting into sales. I got rejected over and over again, with people telling me I looked too young and that I didn't have enough experience. They would ask me if I'd closed any sales, and, at first, I fumbled the answer. But with each rejection I would become a little bit smarter, a little bit stronger, and a whole lot more resilient. My boss told me that sales was all about persistence and follow up, because most people give up: 80 percent of sales require five follow-up calls after a meeting, and only 44 percent of salespeople follow up after the first call.[29] Ultimately, it took me fourteen months to close my first deal. This is how I learned resilience is showing up over and over again even in the face of adversity and rejection: it's about leaning into discomfort and continuing to grow and adapt when faced with any obstacle.

Three ways to Foster Resilience are:

Celebrate Small Wins

> *"Success is rarely the result of one swell swoop, but more often the culmination of many, many small victories."*
> —Joseph M. Marshall III[30]

Acknowledge and appreciate the small achievements along your journey. Celebrating the minor victories reminds you of the progress you've made. Recognizing and celebrating the small wins is crucial for the winner's mindset. Winners always have big aspirations and dreams, and it's easy to skip over the smaller milestones. When winners stay constantly chasing and only seek the big thrills, they lose appreciation for the milestones that are accomplished along the way to achieving the big goal. All progress is measured in increments, and if you can be incrementally better every day, then it's a good day.

---

[29] Brian Williams, PhD, "21 Mind-Blowing Sales Stats," *The Brevet Group* (blog), accessed August 6, 2024, https://blog.thebrevetgroup.com/21-mind-blowing-sales-stats#:~:text=44%25%20of%20sales%20reps%20give,prospect%20post%20your%20initial%20meeting.

[30] "Joseph M. Marshall III Quote: 'Success is rarely the result of one swell swoop, but more often the culmination of many, many small victories.'" Joseph M. Marshall III, Quotefancy, accessed August 6, 2024, https://quotefancy.com/quote/1714214/Joseph-M-Marshall-III-Success-is-rarely-the-result-of-one-swell-swoop-but-more-often-the.

Behaviors to Celebrate Small Wins include:

- **Recognize achievements:** Regularly acknowledge and celebrate minor successes to build momentum and morale.
- **Encourage team celebrations:** Foster a culture where small victories are celebrated collectively.
- **Build on success:** Use small wins as building blocks to achieve larger goals.

Dance Anyway

> *"You don't have to be great to start, but you have to start to be great."*
> —Zig Ziglar[31]

A growth mindset empowers you to take that first step, embrace the learning process, and strive for continuous improvement. Life will inevitably present challenges and difficult times—there will be rainy days, and sometimes there will be very long rainy seasons. So anticipate the rain and dance anyway. Embrace the discomfort, knowing that these moments build character and resilience; this isn't the time to pack it up and quit. Instead, do a rain dance and double down. Keep pushing through because magic happens when you fight through your darkest days. Learn to find joy and motivation even in the most challenging times because pushing through these periods often leads to the most significant personal growth and success.

Behaviors to Dance Anyway include:

---

[31] "Quote by Zig Ziglar: 'You don't have to be great to start, but you have to start to be great.'" Zig Ziglar, Goodreads, accessed August 6, 2024, https://www.goodreads.com/quotes/59427-you-don-t-have-to-be-great-to-start-but-you.

- **Embrace challenges:** Don't settle for what's comfortable; aim for what challenges you.
- **Maintain positivity:** Find joy in adversity by keeping a positive attitude and seeing challenges as opportunities for growth.
- **Persist through setbacks:** Keep pushing forward even during tough times, believing that breakthroughs often come after the most challenging battles. When things don't go as planned, don't give up. Analyze, learn, and try again.

Look Many Ways

"I have no special talent. I am only passionately curious."
—Albert Einstein[32]

Solutions and answers aren't always found in the most obvious places. In fact, you'll find answers by looking in multiple directions, so look up, down, out, and to every angle and side. Explore different angles, consider diverse viewpoints, and remain open-minded. This broad vision can lead to innovative solutions and unexpected opportunities.

Behaviors to Look Many Ways include:

- **Seek diverse perspectives:** Cultivate a habit of looking at situations from multiple angles and encourage diverse viewpoints.

---

[32] "Albert Einstein – I have no special talent. I am only passionately curious." Albert Einstein, BrainyQuote, accessed August 6, 2024, https://www.brainyquote.com/quotes/albert_einstein_174001.

- **Be curious:** Ask questions constantly and look beyond the obvious to find innovative solutions.
- **Expand your vision:** Broaden your scope by considering different possibilities and approaches.

Theme 3: Cultivate a Growth Mindset

> *"The view you adopt for yourself profoundly affects the way you lead your life."*
> —Carol Dweck[33]

Carol Dweck coined the term "Growth Mindset." Her research highlighted that those with a growth mindset—those who believe that abilities can be developed—are much more likely to flourish than people with a fixed mindset—those who believe that abilities are unchangeable.

Embracing a growth mindset allows you to tackle challenges with enthusiasm and resilience rather than fear or hesitation. It empowers you to see obstacles as opportunities to learn and improve, not as threats to your self-worth.

When I was in college, I spent a semester living and studying abroad. I enrolled in a program that allowed me to live in India, Russia, and China while studying emerging business markets. Through studying culture, religion, history, and the geopolitical factors of each country, I was able to get a stronger

---

[33] "Quote by Carol S. Dweck: 'the view you adopt for yourself profoundly affects the way you lead your life. It can determine whether you become the person you want to be and whether you accomplish the things you value.'" Carol Dweck, Goodreads, accessed August 6, 2024, https://www.goodreads.com/quotes/7668154-the-view-you-adopt-for-yourself-profoundly-affects-the-way.

grasp on how deep-seated cultural norms impact global markets and business operations. One of the biggest takeaways I learned during these travels wasn't only to embrace the discomfort I was bound to feel, but to remain curious about every situation and interaction I was exposed to. So I challenged myself to document every instance I had that felt different or uncomfortable and look for the "why" behind it: why is respecting your elders a key component in Chinese culture? How does the dramatic economic divide in India impact political factors? What are the continued and lasting impacts of the Soviet Union on the Russian people? How did three countries and economies booming on the world stage have wildly different attitudes and commerce practices? In India, there are seven hundred different languages, twenty-two of which are recognized by the country as official languages. How does this impact communication within the country? My list of questions was endless. The more I started writing down, the more I realized that I had.

The questions I wrote down in my notebook started changing the conversations I was having through my interactions. I grew more curious about everything, constantly looking for interconnectivity, constantly trying to understand the why, and always trying to put the pieces together. This is the heart of cultivating a growth mindset: asking the questions, seeking the answers, and always remaining curious to learn more and repurpose that knowledge in your life.

Three ways to Cultivate a Growth Mindset are:

Be a Lifelong Learner

> *"Anyone who stops learning is old, whether at twenty or eighty. Anyone who keeps learning stays young."*
> —Henry Ford[34]

Never stop learning and improving. Regardless of your experience or expertise, there's always something new to discover. Cultivate a passion for continuous learning and skill development, because this dedication to growth fuels both personal and professional success. Obsessing over your craft leads to mastery and keeps you ahead in your field, so commit yourself to being a lifelong learner and acknowledge and recognize that you don't know or have all of the answers—and never will.

When you look at life, you have something to gain and learn from every single situation, every single person you encounter, every single day. Each new perspective or fresh skill holds something valuable. Additionally, teaching is an extension of learning—anyone can be a teacher, regardless of age or title, because true teaching comes from a place of understanding. You don't truly grasp a concept until you can explain it to someone else, and in doing so, you reveal both your strengths and areas for growth. The act of teaching itself reinforces learning, creating a powerful cycle of continuous improvement.

---

[34] "Quote by Henry Ford: 'Anyone who stops learning is old, whether at twenty or eighty. Anyone who keeps learning stays young.'" Henry Ford, Goodreads, accessed August 6, 2024, https://www.goodreads.com/quotes/37961-anyone-who-stops-learning-is-old-whether-at-twenty-or.

Behaviors to Be a Lifelong Learner include:

- **Pursue continuous learning:** Embrace opportunities to learn and grow professionally and personally. No matter how long you've been doing something, there's always something new to learn.
- **Encourage peer-to-peer teaching:** Enable employees to share their knowledge and skills with each other. You have to know it to teach it!
- **Model learning behavior:** Share your own learning journey and demonstrate a commitment to skill development. Let obsessing over skill building and the craft drive you.

Flow with Life

> *"Be water, my friend. Empty your mind, be formless, shapeless—like water. Now you put water in a cup, it becomes the cup; you put water into a bottle, it becomes the bottle; you put it in a teapot, it becomes the teapot. Now water can flow or it can crash. Be water, my friend."*
> —Bruce Lee[35]

Like with fishing, you can't resist the current and fight the tide. Instead of resisting change, adapt to it. When you flow with the direction life is pushing you in, you will unlock your most liberated and powerful self. Embrace the direction life takes you and find strength in flexibility.

---

[35] Bruce Lee, *The Warrior Within: The Philosophies of Bruce Lee* (New York City: Chartwell Books, 2016).

MASTERING INTENTIONS

In fishing, oftentimes you can know what you'll be reeling in with the first bite if you're pay attention to the line vibration. It's the same for people: people are exactly who they are; they tend to show their true colors from the start, and you need to pay attention and believe them when they do. By aligning with life's current, you unlock a more liberated and powerful version of yourself, capable of gracefully navigating any situation.

Behaviors to Flow with Life include:

- **Embrace change:** Welcome new directions and adapt to life's natural flow without resistance.
- **Embrace silence:** The best moments of growth happen when you sit still in silence.
- **Stay attuned:** Pay attention to early signals and adjust your actions accordingly. Move in harmony with the energy around you, finding strength and liberation in going with the flow.

Celebrate Failures as Learning Opportunities

"Failure should be our teacher, not our undertaker. Failure is delay, not defeat. It is a temporary detour, not a dead end."
—Denis Waitley[36]

Failure is not the end; it's a brief deviation on the path to success. Shift the team's perception of failure from something to

---

[36] "Quote by Denis Waitley: 'Failure should be our teacher, not our undertaker. Failure is delay, not defeat. It is a temporary detour, not a dead end. Failure is something we can only avoid by saying nothing, doing nothing, and being nothing.'" Denis Waitley, Goodreads, accessed August 6, 2024, https://www.goodreads.com/quotes/79466-failure-should-be-our-teacher-not-our-undertaker-failure-is.

be avoided to something to learn from. Every setback carries valuable lessons that can propel you forward if you approach them with an open mind and a willingness to learn. When mistakes are made, analyze what went wrong and how the team can improve moving forward. By embracing failure as a natural part of the growth process, you cultivate resilience and foster an environment where innovation and creativity can thrive. The key to celebrating failure lies in the ability to see beyond the immediate disappointment and recognize the potential for growth and improvement.

When failure occurs, it's easy to fall into the trap of self-criticism or blame. However, shifting the narrative from failure as a negative outcome to a learning opportunity empowers individuals and teams to continue to take risks, experiment, and push boundaries. This mindset shift is crucial for both personal and professional development. Embracing failure also encourages transparency, collaboration, and a culture where everyone feels safe to share their mistakes and insights.

Behaviors to Celebrate Failures as Learning Opportunities include:

- **Encourage a reflective mindset:** After any setback, take the time to reflect on what went wrong and why. Encourage team members to analyze their failures constructively, focusing on the lessons learned rather than the mistakes made. Facilitate discussions that promote understanding and growth.
- **Promote a culture of experimentation:** Create an environment where risk-taking is encouraged and failures are seen as an inevitable part of the innovation process. Celebrate attempts to innovate, even when

they don't succeed, and recognize the value in the effort and lessons that come from trying something new.
- **Share lessons learned:** Make it a practice to openly share the insights gained from failures with the team. This could be through regular team meetings, retrospectives, or informal discussions. By sharing these experiences, you can help others avoid similar pitfalls and build a collective knowledge base that strengthens the team.

A Winner's Mindset is About Positive Energy

A Winner's Mindset is about recognizing that not everything is in your control. In fact, most of life isn't in your control. However, by remaining true to your core values, having intent in your action, surrendering to life's plan, learning the lessons, and adjusting as needed with confidence, you will always come out on top as a winner. While the win may not be exactly what you envisioned—while it may seem like a "loss" to others—for winners, there's always a win; it's simply a matter of perspective. The lessons life is teaching us are ever present once we start paying attention. Even as a winner, no matter how good I am or how well I'm doing, I have the humility to know that I can still do more; I balance my humility with my pride.

A Winner's Mindset is about putting your headspace in a position to believe that you're a winner and that anything is possible. It fuels optimism. With it there is opportunity every day, and with every experience and interaction. It possesses a spirit that a former professor of mine, Professor Kevin Mulcahy, described as "it's not a question of whether the glass is half full or half empty, but a perspective that the glass is simply not big enough."

Understanding Toxic Positivity

You might have heard the term toxic positivity in the context of social media or by means of well-meaning advice from friends. Toxic positivity is the belief that no matter how dire or difficult a situation is, one should maintain a positive mindset and dismiss any negative emotions. While positivity is generally a good thing, toxic positivity takes it to an extreme. It denies people the right to feel hurt, angry, or sad, and it forces a smile on situations where genuine emotional responses are necessary for growth and healing.

Imagine being told, "Just stay positive!" when you're going through a tough breakup, or "Everything happens for a reason!" when you lose a loved one. These statements, though well-intentioned, can be dismissive and invalidating. They don't leave room for the complex, often painful emotions that are a natural part of the human experience. Toxic positivity can create an environment where people feel compelled to suppress their true feelings, which can lead to deeper emotional issues down the line. It can also stem from a place of insecurity or fear. We might tell ourselves, "I have to stay positive because if I don't, I'll fall apart," or "I can't let anyone see me struggle; it would mean I'm weak." Toxic positivity becomes truly toxic when we cling to it because we're afraid of confronting the darker, more difficult aspects of our life.

Practicing Contagious Positivity

So, how can we practice positivity in a healthy, constructive way, rather than a toxic one? Instead of forcing ourselves or others to "just be positive," we can focus on acknowledging the reality of our situations while maintaining hope and faith in our ability to navigate them.

I use the term *Contagious Positivity* to describe this practice of spreading optimism and hope while acknowledging and respecting the reality of challenges. It combines a positive mindset with authenticity, encouraging resilience and honest emotional expression.

For example, if you're going through a tough time, it's okay to admit that things are hard. You can say, "I'm really struggling right now, but I know I've overcome challenges before, and I'm proud of the progress I'm making, even if it's slow." This approach lets you be honest about your feelings while maintaining a positive outlook.

When I act with contagious positivity, I do so with an inner belief that things will eventually work out, but *without denying* the difficulties I face along the way. It's about trusting the process of life, staying the course, and continuing to be the best versions of ourselves. This doesn't mean ignoring our problems or pretending everything is perfect. Instead, it means embracing the full spectrum of our emotions and taking pride in our ability to navigate them.

Let me give you an example of being action-oriented around positivity. In 2023, the New York City real estate market had its worst year in over twenty years. While some chose to be in a frenzy and freak out, there was another option available: being action-oriented, focused, and optimistic that the market would turn around. I told my team that if we best positioned our product, remained aggressive, continued doing our marketing efforts, corrected our pricing, and got ahead of the curve, we would continue to transact. Even if it wasn't the solution we'd hoped for, I made a point to emphasize that there's always a way out of the situation and that *we could still act*.

Don't avoid action because it's not the action you desire to take. After all, action is a prerequisite for movement, and movement is a prerequisite for getting positive outcomes. I always win business because of my energy. My positive outlook is this: if we stay on course and continue to put in the work, then everything will work out precisely the way it should. It doesn't mean we take our foot off the pedal. It doesn't mean we stop working. We still have to do all of those things, but if all the pieces are aligned, we must trust the process. It's this energy that makes me believe that everything is alright, everything will be okay, and everything will work itself out.

Practice Positive Reinforcement

Here are some ways you can practice contagious positivity via positive reinforcement:

- When people ask me "How are you doing?" I respond with, "I'm doing great because today will be a great day." If you tell yourself that it's going to be a great day and everything's going to work out, it will.
- Start speaking positively to everybody and about everything. If you don't have something positive or nice to say, don't say it.

- Don't be blindly positive; there's a difference between being positive and being disillusioned. It's one thing to be whimsical about it and say everything will work itself out and another to be intentional and action-oriented.

Contagious Positivity is Sticky

Contagious positivity spreads fast. It spreads the moment somebody else acts positively because then you act positively; people can feel it. You can't be positive about yourself and *not* impact change, so dare to spread that around. In every interaction that we have with someone, we can leave them feeling better, worse, or neutral depending on what we say to them and what observations we made. Do you want to pump them up, drag them down, or not see them at all? Ask yourself: are you a positive person? Do you treat other people positively? How do you respond to positivity?

A Winner's Mindset Expresses Pride

Pride is often viewed in a negative light, especially when we think of it in terms of arrogance or vanity. However, I believe pride is a healthy, constructive force. For me, pride is the feeling of satisfaction I get from my achievements and the recognition of the hard work I've put in.

Pride, in its healthiest form, is about self-respect. It's about recognizing that we've accomplished something meaningful or have overcome a difficult situation, and acknowledging our effort and progress. It motivates us, boosts our confidence, and drives us to take on new challenges.

Sometimes we forget how long we've been working at something, what that moment of accomplishment looked like, and all the things we had to do to get there. Take a moment to look inward at when and where you felt proud of yourself—that feeling of inner pride is an internal source of energy; you can't take it away from someone. When somebody's feeling proud, it shows. Personally, I've found it beneficial to take personal pride in my growth because it helps me continue to push my boundaries.

Exercise 5.1: What Made Me Proud?

Step 1: What Made Me Proud?

Look back at the previous six months and name five things that you're most proud of, then ask yourself:

- Why am I most proud of those things?
- How did they make me feel when they happened?
- How did they make me feel afterward?

Step 2: What Did I Learn?

Document and review your answers to these questions and go one step further, asking:

- Did I manifest or intentionally set out to do any of these things?
- How did these become proud moments or achievements in my life?

Examining your intentionality and how these moments came about can help you tune into the types of accomplishments that shape your feelings of genuine pride. This, in turn, can help you decide where you direct your energy as new opportunities arise.

When I did this with my team, I remember one woman told me, "One of my proudest moments in the past six months was when my son got up on stage at the school concert and was able to sing the song that he had been working on, even though he had terrible stage fright." She was so proud of that because she worked really hard with her young son to give him the confidence he needed to overcome his stage fright. They practiced together every night, and seeing his excitement and how happy he was made her proud of how hard she'd to help get him there. It was a very self-validating moment.

You can be proud of what you've done and proud of what others have done, too. In its healthiest form, my pride is about recognizing and appreciating the collective efforts and progress of my team and acknowledging the hard work and perseverance that led to our achievements. Ultimately, pride is constructive: it motivates us, boosts our confidence, and gives us the energy to tackle challenges.

The Intersection of Contagious Positivity and Pride

Where do contagious positivity and pride intersect? The answer lies in how we respond to challenges and perceive our own worth. It's okay to not be okay at times, to struggle, to feel lost, and to ask for help. What's important is that we don't lose sight of our inherent worth and the progress we've made. By embracing both contagious positivity and pride, we can lead lives that are fulfilling and resilient. If we allow ourselves to experience and express genuine emotions—including the negative ones—we're also allowing ourselves to be vulnerable.

Healthy pride encourages us to acknowledge our emotions and take pride in our resilience. It's about saying, "Yes, this is hard, and I'm struggling, but I'm proud of myself for facing this challenge head-on." It's not about pretending that everything is fine when it's not; it's about recognizing our capacity to endure and grow through adversity. Combining a positive outlook with a healthy pride creates a powerful force that can help us overcome challenges and achieve our goals.

Overcoming Past Trauma and Embracing Growth: A Foundation of Resilience

Reliving years of trauma (including those years of being depressed), I realized that even when I mentally didn't have the strength to, I was able to find the fight to survive. If I was able to overcome that, realize and recognize what happiness was, and find hope on the other side then, I know I'll find that in *whatever* moment I'm struggling with I can survive.

Each of us carries the weight of our experiences, both the joyous and the painful. Trauma, in particular, can leave a lasting impact, shaping how we see the world and how we respond to challenges. But here's the remarkable thing about trauma: when you confront it, when you allow yourself to relive and process those difficult experiences, you begin to develop a strength that's unparalleled. It becomes a part of your muscle memory, enabling you to react with resilience—almost on autopilot.

Think of it this way: the more you face your trauma head-on, the more you reduce the time it takes to bounce back from adversity. You begin to recognize that something that could break you today will no longer have the same power over you if you continue fighting, pushing, and persevering. This shift in perspective is what I call an inflection point, a moment in which your whole life—including your business and relationships—starts to change for the better. It's the realization that you have the power to overcome anything, and that realization sets the stage for growth, change, and positivity.

From a Resilient to a Growth Mindset

This resilience, this ability to bounce back, naturally leads to the development of a growth mindset. As we discussed earlier in this practice, a growth mindset is the belief that you never have all the answers and that there's no single, clear path to success. Instead, it's about recognizing that life is a continuous journey of learning, adapting, and evolving. It's about embracing the uncertainty of not knowing everything and being okay with it because you're committed to learning.

Contrast this with a fixed mindset—the belief that failure is the end of the road, that you have all the answers, or that you're somehow superior to others. A fixed mindset traps you in a cycle of negativity, preventing growth and stifling innovation. It keeps you from seeing failure as an opportunity to learn and evolve. In contrast, someone with a growth mindset sees every failure as a building block, a chance to grow stronger and more capable.

Emotional Regulation is Key to Navigating Life's Highs and Lows

Another crucial aspect of developing a growth mindset is emotional regulation, which is incredibly challenging, especially in a world filled with uncertainty. As you progress on your professional journey, you'll find that your highs will feel exhilarating, and your lows will feel devastating. When you learn to regulate your emotions and balance out the extremes, however, you'll start to trust the process of life. You'll begin to see that not everything is the end or the beginning, but rather *everything is simply part of the journey.*

Emotional regulation allows you to make clearer, more rational decisions and helps you relate to others on a deeper level. It's about staying calm in the face of adversity and recognizing that every challenge is an opportunity for growth. So, how do you develop this skill?

Practice Mindfulness

Deep breathing, taking time to reflect before reacting, and never responding in the heat of anger is a great place to start. Role-playing difficult conversations in your head before having them can also help you approach situations with more clarity and confidence.

Surround Yourself with a Positive Support System

One of the most important things you can do as you navigate the ups and downs of life is to build a strong support system. But it's not enough to surround yourself with friends and family; you need a support system of like-minded individuals who challenge you to think positively and approach failure with a growth mindset. The energy of the people you surround yourself with is contagious. If you're around negativity, it will seep into your mindset and outlook on life. But if you're surrounded by positivity, you'll be inspired to grow, innovate, and push through challenges.

Lead with Contagious Positivity and a Growth Mindset

As you step into leadership roles—whether in your career or personal life—the question becomes: how do you use these skills to lead? How do you create impact, build teams, and foster an environment where others can also thrive? The answer lies in embedding a growth mindset as a core value of your leadership.

Promote a Growth Mindset

Create a culture around you where failure is not feared, but embraced as a learning opportunity. Encourage your team to lean into challenges, fail forward, and grow from every experience. Doing so creates an environment where people are connected not just to the organization, but to their own personal growth journeys. This connection fosters resilience, innovation, and a drive to achieve greatness.

Summary of Practice 5: Adopt a Winner's Mindset

To have a winner's mindset, you must have experienced loss. You must have faced challenges and setbacks to understand what it means to push forward and truly win. Resilience, at its core, is about how you bounce back from adversity. It's not about allowing losses to define you, but using them as fuel to become better. Your last loss doesn't define you, and it should *never* dictate your future. Instead, it should propel you to try harder, push further, and strive for success.

If you're always winning, you're not playing the right game. True growth happens when you're challenged—when you're out of your comfort zone and striving to achieve what seems impossible. So, seek out challenges that push you beyond your limits. Embrace the discomfort that comes with growth, because it's through discomfort that you learn, evolve, and ultimately, succeed.

Embrace the growth mindset advocated by Carol Dweck, cultivate resilience, and surround yourself with positivity. Lead with authenticity and vulnerability, and never stop striving to learn, grow, and become the best version of yourself.

Your past doesn't define you—your resilience, growth, and ability to overcome challenges do. So go out there, embrace the discomfort, and trust in the process of life. The future is ours to shape, and we're each capable of doing extraordinary things by our own definitions of extraordinary. The most powerful leaders are those who lead with both their heads and their hearts, so be bold, be brave, and most importantly, be yourself.

Implications for Innerwork:

- Accept your vulnerabilities as a source of strength, allowing yourself to grow and connect more authentically with others.
- Build resilience by celebrating small wins, facing challenges with determination, and viewing setbacks as opportunities for growth.
- Continuously seek learning opportunities and remain curious.

- View obstacles as chances to expand your capabilities.
- Develop emotional regulation to navigate the highs and lows of life.
- Bear in mind, our last loss doesn't define us; how we rise from it does.
- Practice contagious positivity to shape your mood and that of those around you.

Implications for Teamship:

- Encourage a culture where team members feel safe to express their vulnerabilities, fostering trust and stronger relationships within the team.
- Celebrate small victories.
- View failures as valuable learning experiences.
- Cultivate a team culture that embraces continuous learning and encourages experimentation.
- Build a support system within the team that emphasizes emotional regulation, helping members to stay balanced and resilient in the face of challenges.
- Lead by example in practicing authenticity and contagious positivity, inspiring the team to maintain a positive outlook while addressing real challenges.

Practice 6

MANIFEST YOUR FUTURE

Trust in yourself that what you manifest will one day become reality.

Manifestation is a superpower—it's certainly mine. Above anything else I've done or practiced, the moment I realized that my mind is the greatest gift and the most powerful force in the world, everything began to change. Your mind controls your perception of reality as it currently stands, as well as what's possible for the future. Therefore, when you begin to move through the world with intention, a clear vision, and a destination in sight, opportunities will start arising, circumstances will change, and the right people will enter your life to join you on the journey.

Before starting my company, I had partners in another real estate business. When we started the partnership, it felt like we were the right partners, at the right time, and for the right reason. Many aspects of the business gelled and worked, but there were also a few red flags that I kept pushing down and trying to ignore. It was my first business, and unfortunately it was no surprise to me when the partnership imploded and massively failed. I remember the feeling in my gut when I knew something was off—it wasn't right. I knew that if I was building something from scratch, I wanted it to feel different. I wanted it to be challenging but fantastic, powerful, magnetic, and hard. So I started manifesting that feeling. I wanted it to feel electric and intoxicating, like everything I was building and creating made me yearn for more. I didn't know what that looked like, but I knew what it felt like. It was an energy I created, and I knew that anything would be possible if I could possess that feeling.

When I look back on it now, I call that my CEO manifestation. I would wake up every morning, lay in bed, and think about what life would look like. What it would feel like to work around people who I cared about and who inspired me so profoundly. I would go to bed and think about how tired I wish I felt because I was building the life of my dreams. I would feel everything. I would be there knowing that it was happening and that I was building it. Every day, waking up and going to bed, visualizing walking to work knowing I was going to my office, walking through the door and seeing my company logo on the wall, greeting my staff as they came in knowing they were sharing in my vision, and meeting with and pitching clients knowing they were getting the quality of service only I could deliver. I would imagine every scenario I wanted, and I put myself there, day after day. Six months later, when the partnership ended, I knew it was my time—this was the moment.

It took another six months to figure out how to execute the feelings of the dreams I had been visualizing. After two years of continuing to visualize and manifest, I kept powering through. I experienced tons of failures and countless setbacks, but I kept forging ahead. I didn't feel it yet, but I was working towards it, and then the things I'd visualized started happening one by one: how good it felt to walk to work excited to enter my office, and what was once two of us turned into four, then six, then eight. I remember holding the first piece of merchandise we made for the company. While our logo was already on the signage, in print, and online, I remember holding the first sweatshirt we made. That was the feeling I had been dreaming about: my logo was there, in print, embroidered on a sweatshirt. It was a moment of pride and I had an incredible sense of accomplishment.

The team kept growing and the business kept expanding. The calls started coming in, and instead of us chasing after business, the business started coming to us. I remember when we signed up for our first $60 million project after starting the company and thinking to myself, "This is it; this is the first big one." I knew it would happen and knew the feeling I would feel when it did because I'd forced myself to feel it before I knew it was even possible. One project turned into three, which eventually turned into forty development projects. The feeling—the euphoria—it still feels the same, every single time. It feels the way I always knew it would feel—*that is manifestation.*

The practice of manifestation has made a profound difference in my life. It's become such a strong force that I now experience the powers of my manifestation almost every single day: in the relationships I have, in the experiences I enjoy, and in the successes I celebrate. The powers of manifestation can be around you in everything you do—you just have to get clarity and get started.

What is Manifestation?

Manifestation is bringing your desires into reality through focused intention, belief, and aligned action. It's based on the idea that your thoughts, feelings, and beliefs influence the world around you. It's about understanding the deep connection between your inner world and your outer reality.

Key Principles of Manifestation

Manifestation is about creating a life that feels fulfilling, joyful, and aligned with your deepest values and aspirations. It's about becoming the person you want to be and living the life you desire. Manifestation is a holistic practice that touches every aspect of your life, from your relationships and careers to your personal growth and overall well-being. Three fundamental principles shape my own manifestation practices:

1. The Law of Attraction

Whether positive or negative, whatever we focus on expands and becomes our reality. Put another way, "Like attracts like." When we constantly worry about what could go wrong, we're potentially inviting occurrences of Murphy's Law—anything that can go wrong, will go wrong.[37] In contrast, when we focus with clarity and belief on what we want, we begin to attract more positive outcomes into our lives. That's because when you put energy into the universe, you attract that same energy. If you put positive energy into the world daily, positive things will

---

[37] *Merriam-Webster*, s.v., "Murphy's Law (n.)," accessed August 10, 2024, https://www.merriam-webster.com/dictionary/Murphy%27s%20Law.

return to you. This doesn't mean you won't experience hardship, but holistically, positive things will come your way.

On the flip side, when you put negative energy or opposing forces out into the world, life will feel more strenuous and tense. The energy you put into the universe is directly related to your mental state. For example, when you're constantly anxious, sad, or frustrated, you tend to look at everything with a glass half empty mentality. In turn, you start to attract those negative forces into your life. These are the "woe is me" people who constantly ask, "Why does this keep happening to me? Why is life so difficult? Why does nothing go my way?" Because that's the energy they're putting out there—and therefore what they're attracting. If that's your mentality, then you'll continue to live in that cycle.

2. The Power of Belief

Manifestation requires us to believe that our desires can and will come true (even when there's no immediate evidence to support that belief!). Belief is a powerful force. It acts like a magnet, drawing our desires closer to us. When we deeply believe in the possibility of something, our thoughts, emotions, and actions naturally align with that belief, creating the conditions for it to manifest in our lives. An important distinction to make is between the power of belief versus hope. Hope is wishing that things will get better or will change, whereas belief is knowing that they will. It's active, intentional, and definitive. "I believe" feels and sounds a lot different than "I hope." Belief is strong—it possesses conviction and trust.

3. The Process of Becoming

Manifestation isn't just about what we bring into our lives, but also about how we're transformed. It's about being both our reality's "creator" and "experiencer." This perspective emphasizes the interconnectedness of actively creating our reality and being shaped by the outcomes. The process of becoming is using our past experiences to shape and mold our future ones.

The Feelings Behind Manifestation

One of the most essential aspects of manifestation is the feelings behind it. The emotions we associate with our desires are what drive the manifestation process. It's not enough to think about what we want; we need to feel it viscerally and deeply as if it's already ours.

Many people get stuck in this situation because they focus on the absence of what they want rather than the feeling of having it. When we focus on lack, we create more of it. But when we focus on the feeling of abundance, joy, or love, we attract more experiences that resonate with those emotions.

The aligning actions we've discussed after each practice are ways we can spend time each day connecting with the emotions of our desired outcomes. If you're manifesting a new job, imagine the excitement of starting your first day, the satisfaction of doing work you love, and the joy of financial stability. If you're manifesting a loving relationship, feel the warmth, connection, and happiness that come with it. The more we immerse ourselves in these feelings, the more we attract them into our lives. When we're in a positive state of mind, we're naturally more open to receiving good things. Intentionally surround yourself with people and activities that make you feel good and invest in regular self-care to keep your energy high. Be receptive to how aligning actions shape both your inner and outer realities.

Exercise 6.1: Key Practices of Manifestation

Several fundamental, tried-and-true practices can be easily incorporated into your daily routine. The key to manifestation is consistency, so block time to make these practices a regular part of your life.

Aligning actions—which we'll talk about more in a bit—is one way we can spend time connecting with the emotions of our desired outcomes each day. The starting point to begin incorporating manifestation into your life is to think about your mental state: success lies in understanding the current state of your mental health and what steps you can take to improve it. There's no judgment about where your starting point is—enhancing and improving your mental state is very similar to improving your physical health and just as, if not even more, important. The goal is to get healthier and better from where we are today by committing ourselves to small steps and daily practices to improve slowly over time. Utilizing the principles of manifestation, we can begin to improve the state of our mental well-being, and here's how:

1. Set Clear Intentions

You can set intentions for anything, but at the most basic level, you should be setting your intentions for the day, especially how you start your day in the morning and your attitude when you wake up. I wake up every day truly grateful to be alive. Why?

Because I suffered for a very long time wishing that I wasn't. When I think about it, when I get out of bed every morning, I feel blessed to be here. Even when I'm going through challenging seasons of life, I come back to this feeling to make sure I start my day with gratitude and positivity because I know very well what it's like to live without those feelings.

Starting your day on the right foot helps you continue the day in the right trajectory. If you wake up grumpy or angry, it's so much harder to turn your day around as it moves on. It will also be harder to overcome setbacks, obstacles, and friction that arise throughout the day because your mental state won't be at its strongest when coping and responding to these situations. Now I'm not saying you need to bounce out of bed and start singing a musical—although this *is* what I do on days when I'm a little more tired than usual and struggling to move my body. I recognize we're not all morning people; however, you can still start your day with positive energy even if you're not.

As a business owner, I manage people and am in a market-based industry. This means that at some point in my morning I *will* experience a frustrated client, a stressed-out employee, and a deal or two will start to go off the rails. With that being said, I know that if I start my day with mental clarity and on a positive note, I'm better equipped to handle these conversations and obstacles and will be a much stronger problem solver because I'll be responding with intent, not with emotion. Conversely, if I were to start the day off angry, unrested, frustrated or without clarity, *everything* would start to amplify and compound and by the end of the day, I would feel completely out of control. This is why I start my day with clear intentions and focus on moving them forward. By the end of the day, I know I'll have taken steps to improve my mental health.

Aligning Actions

Remember, manifestation begins with being clear on what you want. However, many people struggle with this clarity of intention because they haven't thought through their core desires in detail. So first spend some time reflecting on what you truly want in the different areas of your life: your career, health, personal growth, relationships, and so on. Write these down as clear, specific intentions—the more detailed, the better. Clarity will help you focus your energy and attention on what matters most to you. For example, instead of saying, "I want to be successful," try to define what success looks like for you. Is it having a fulfilling career? Building meaningful relationships? Achieving financial independence? The more specific you are, the easier it will be to visualize and manifest your desires. Your clear intentions serve as an aspirational roadmap to guide you toward your goals with purpose and direction.

2. Visualize

For you to manifest, you need to see and feel yourself as the person willing to accomplish or able to achieve what you're setting out to do. The visualization and feeling technique is very powerful because your body, mind, and heart need to be open to accepting and recognizing that you deserve good things when they come your way. Personally, when I visualize, it's very important for me to close my eyes and put myself in that specific situation, in that particular setting, and walk through all of the motions, like playing it out in a movie.

In December 2022, I was fourteen months into starting my current company. I remember sitting down at my desk and visualizing what I wanted the next chapter of the business to look like. I was reflecting on all of the sources of joy I had found over the past year and what excited me most. I was just starting to ramp up with speaking opportunities, including panels, Q and As, and participating in various industry conferences. I had never been on a stage alone, but decided I wanted to try. I put into the universe that I would deliver a keynote speech one day, I started dreaming about it and visualizing myself there on that stage. I would sit down with my eyes closed and feel the jitters I would have before walking on stage, breathing through the anxiety of walking up the steps, feeling the lights on me, and starting to speak. I would imagine what it would feel like looking down into the crowd and seeing faces looking up at me and nodding, smiling, and agreeing with what I was saying. I focused on the feeling I would have connecting with hundreds of people through sharing my stories.

On the morning of January 25, 2023, I was getting ready to speak on a side stage panel at Inman Connect, a large real estate conference in New York City. My phone rang, and it was a past client of mine, one who I'd worked with two years prior and hadn't spoken with much since.

I answered, and she started talking about a conference she was hosting in Dubai and asked if I had any experience and was comfortable speaking on stage. I told her I was actually getting ready to speak at the Inman Connect conference and said, "Of course I'm comfortable, I love speaking on stage!"

She asked if I was open to traveling, if I was free in three weeks, and if I would come to Dubai and speak at their conference. If I was going to be considered, I needed to put together a speaker reel and send it to her by the end of the week since the conference was less than thirty days out. I was so excited that I quickly said yes and promised she would have a speaker reel by the end of the week.

As soon as I hung up with her, I immediately rallied my troops, "Today, we're going to film a speaker reel at the conference. We leave in an hour."

The next day, she had the iPhone footage my assistant filmed, and the day after that, she called me and said, "You've got it. You need to be in Dubai on February 12th."

Without even consulting my calendar, I gave another quick response, "I'll be there."

When I landed in Dubai, my first stop was the convention center. Wow—this was it; I was traveling internationally to speak. Was this what I'd dreamed of? When I arrived, I picked up the program for the conference to find my name listed as the keynote speaker. My jaw dropped to the floor.

My best friend, who was traveling with me and standing beside me, whispered, "Did you know you were giving the keynote?" I shook my head no in silence. We exchanged glances for a minute, and when we walked out of the cold conference center and back into the Dubai heat, the panic started to hit.

I knew I was here to speak, but to give the keynote speech? I was not prepared for this. I kept replaying our phone conversation and asking myself, "Did she tell me I was giving the keynote?" It didn't matter at this point because I was giving it, and now it was up to me. Naturally, my Brain Bully was louder than ever:

> *"You aren't prepared."*
> *"You aren't qualified."*
> *"You've never done this before."*
> *"You are tired."*
> *"You are jetlagged."*

And then the self-talk started:

"Bianca, cut it out."
"I'm ready."
"I'm prepared."
"They asked me. I'm here. So, I must be qualified."
"I can do this."
"I've dreamed of this."
"I will do this."
"I will pour my heart out on that stage."
"I will give this everything I have."
"Now is your time."

Everything I'd dreamed of, everything I'd manifested—it was here, it was happening, and this was the moment.

I'd played this moment over so many times in my head already. I simulated the event. I was the main character in the movie I was playing on repeat. So even when my Brain Bully told me "No, you're not ready," I knew that of course I was ready. I knew how this movie ended because I'd already written it.

When the alarm went off at 5:00 a.m. the morning of my keynote, I immediately jumped out of bed. I was a ball of excitement and a bundle of nerves trying to move my body fast enough so the jetlag wouldn't catch up to me. As I sat in the chair getting my hair and makeup done, I kept reciting what I wanted to say. For me, the first thirty seconds on stage are the scariest because the delivery of the first story after walking on stage is the most important one. Those first thirty seconds set the tone for the next twenty-nine minutes that follow. I squirmed in my chair as the artist contoured my face and I continued mouthing the words with the hand gestures that accompanied.

When I arrived at the conference center I was in a daze. The anxiety really set in once I saw the stage and two thousand chairs set up—I had never spoken in front of this many people before. As people came up to me to introduce themselves, I couldn't remember a single person's name seconds after they said it. I just kept thinking about that first thirty seconds. As the conference started and I sat in the crowd for the first two hours, I didn't hear a single word the speakers said, I only paid attention to their feet. "What if I trip?" I thought. "Okay, Bianca, don't trip, walk slowly, one step at a time." As each speaker and panel concluded, my place in line kept moving up.

Finally, I was next on deck. My hands were shaking as I stood backstage waiting for my name to be announced. This was it. It was time. One step at a time. Don't trip. Thirty seconds. A perfect thirty seconds, that was my focus. As I walked to my mark—a small X on the ground—I looked up and was blinded by the lights. It's incredible how much heat those lights give off. I took a deep breath, smiled, and started. A few minutes later, as the lights became less blinding, faces in the crowd started to appear. They were smiling, they were nodding. It was exactly how I pictured it. Exactly how I manifested it. "Keep going, Bianca, you've got this." My body started to loosen up as I began walking from one side of the stage to the other, trying to best activate the crowd. I looked down at the timer, twelve minutes to go. Did I have enough to say to fill the time? "Bianca, keep going. You're talking about what you do and love to do every single day. Just keep speaking." Finally, I hit the clicker to my final slide, and as I said "Thank you," my heart sank into my chest. The crowd clapped, and some people even stood. As I walked down the stairs, just as slowly and carefully as I walked up them, a crowd of people started to move towards me and I thought to myself, "Wow, I did it."

I left everything I had on that stage—and that was just the beginning of my public speaking manifestation journey. Now, having spoken in front of tens of thousands of people around the world, each time it's exactly as I imagined it would be.

As this experience exemplifies, visualization is a crucial part of the manifestation process—you can't manifest without it. Close your eyes and imagine what it would feel like to achieve your goals. See the details, hear the sounds, and feel the emotions. The key is to fully immerse yourself in the experience, allowing yourself to feel the joy, excitement, and gratitude of having what you want. Visualization helps to align your subconscious mind with your desires, making them feel more natural and attainable.

Aligning Actions

To enhance your visualization practice, create a "mental movie" of your desired outcome. Imagine a scene where you're living your dream life—whether it's receiving a promotion, traveling to a dream destination, or enjoying a fulfilling relationship. Play this movie in your mind regularly, especially in the morning when you wake up and at night before you go to sleep. Over time, this practice will reinforce your belief in your ability to manifest your desires.

3. Make Affirmations

Affirmations are positive, present tense statements that reinforce one's belief in one's ability to manifest one's desires. They're a powerful way to reprogram one's subconscious mind by replacing limiting beliefs with empowering ones.

Remember the positive self-talk practice? This comes into play here. Positive affirmations are a statement of recognition and ownership of something that you possess in yourself that you're declaring to the world. When you deliver a positive affirmation, it's important to identify something you feel good about or want to have, then declare it and own it. For example:

> "I will get the promotion."
> "I will have financial freedom."
> "I will provide for my family."
> "I will see the northern lights."
> "I will get into my dream school."

Aligning Actions

Repeat your affirmations daily, especially in the morning and before bed, when your mind is most receptive. Choose affirmations that resonate with you and feel believable. For example:

- If you're manifesting self-love, you might say, "I am worthy of love and kindness, and I treat myself with compassion every day."
- If you're manifesting career success, you might say, "I attract opportunities that align with my skills and purpose, and I excel in everything I pursue."

This will take some getting used to. Find an aspiration that's a stretch goal! If saying "I'm wealthy" feels too far-fetched, consider starting with "I'm attracting opportunities for financial abundance." As you build confidence in your manifestation practice, adjust your affirmations to reflect your growing belief in your ability to create your desired reality.

4. Practice Gratitude

No matter what's happening in our lives, what season we're in, what heartbreak we're enduring or what financial stress we're overcoming, we all have things in our life to be grateful for. Not everything is all bad all the time, and not everything is all good all the time. There's always good and bad—highs and lows—in all seasons of life. Gratitude is a matter of perspective; it's a discipline of finding, bringing attention to, focusing on, and having an appreciation for the good despite any circumstance. It can be as small as saying "I'm grateful to feel the sun on my face today."

Once you implement practices of gratitude, your positivity for life will begin to change. It will force you—and create muscle memory—to become a glass half-full type of person. Whatever it is, begin to take moments to feel thankful and appreciative. By vocalizing or writing down what you're grateful for, you'll start to live in a state of gratitude.

When my father got in legal trouble, I remember how hard it was to stay positive and keep pushing forward. I felt defeated and in an overwhelming amount of pain that my future would never be what I thought it could be. I remember thinking my family would never be the same and we would never recover. I remember trying so hard to fight for him, but unfortunately, we can't live other people's lives for them—we can't fight their fights, overcome their demons, or want something for them that they don't want for themselves. That's when I forced myself to find gratitude. Even though everything was changing, even though I knew it would never be the same, I just kept thinking to myself "He's alive. My family is healthy and they are here."

Using this practice I started to turn anger, frustration, and resentment into gratitude. I started reframing the situation: him getting into trouble and going to prison was what saved his life. It also deepened my relationships with other companions in my life who were also impacted, including my grandparents and siblings. I became grateful that he was sentenced to seventy-two months and not the maximum sentence of twenty-five years. I was grateful I got to visit him for a few hours on the weekends and that our time was uninterrupted. I was grateful that he was forced to exercise and focus on his own mental health while he was incarcerated. I was grateful he would become a stronger, better person for having had this experience, and I was grateful that I would, too.

Take a minute to think about how it feels to be around someone who's grateful or who actively takes time to express their gratitude. You'll notice that you want to be around those grateful people—I know I do. I feel more connected to grateful people; they excite me. I know we're aligned and I want to grab onto their energy. They're more pleasant to be around than someone who's ungrateful or unappreciative.

Gratitude is a powerful way to attract more positive experiences into your life. By focusing on what you're grateful for, you shift your energy from a "state of lack" to a "state of abundance." Gratitude not only helps you manifest your desires, but it also improves your overall well-being. When you habitually notice and appreciate the good things in your life, you train your brain to focus on positivity, which can lead to better mental and emotional health. Plus, gratitude opens your heart and mind to receive more blessings, making it a powerful tool in manifestation.

Aligning Actions

Start a daily gratitude practice by writing down three things you're grateful for. These don't have to be big things; sometimes, the smallest joys have the greatest impact. This practice will help you develop a more positive outlook and attract more of what you appreciate into your life.

5. Act in Alignment

Thinking and feeling get us started, but manifestation is also about doing. Acting in alignment means making decisions consistent with our desires and intentions. When we talk about acting in alignment, it's helpful to think about the balance between taking action and being shaped by those actions.

To act in alignment not only requires action, it also requires the participation and engagement of others. If you have companions in your life who don't support your manifestations, it will be increasingly harder to achieve them. If your manifestations include various companion partners as part of your journey, it's important to communicate and involve them in your manifestation. For setting career aspirations, family planning, and financial goals, communicating is essential within the family unit. For business milestones and achievements, incorporating your team and work companions is critical to ensure there's alignment.

For the majority of my twenties and into my thirties, I would manifest having great physical health. When I was younger—and when I used to set toxic, metric-specific goals—I would manifest how I would feel when I got on the scale and see the number of the desired weight I wanted to be. I would try to align my actions by having accountability partners and creating healthy eating and exercise goals for myself. For years I disappointed myself, but I didn't stop coming back to this feeling of wanting to look and feel strong—I was just going about it the wrong way.

A few years ago, after my health had really deteriorated, I knew it was time to stop thinking about it and that I needed to actually take action if I wanted this goal, this aspiration, this manifestation to come true. I started by communicating my intentions and alignments with the companions I was spending the most time with and who it would impact most: my work companions. I let them know I wanted to become healthier and stronger for myself and for the business, and in order to do that, I would change my morning routine in order to prioritize working out. I would also be going home earlier so that I could prioritize sleep, which would force us to shift the way we were hosting and entertaining our clients from dinners out to lunches. While my goal of getting healthier was extremely personal, I knew the behaviors and actions that it would require from me would impact my team and possibly business. Therefore, in order to finally make an attempt at being successful and not feel guilty that it was hurting other aspects of my life and career, I needed to get my work companions in alignment with the new actions I would be implementing.

Over the course of the next two years, through daily consistency and actively moving towards the feeling of becoming physically strong, I was able to lose over forty pounds and become the healthiest version of myself—something I never could have done without the support of my companions and the alignment of our actions. I refer to this as my "glow up" manifestation.

Alignment in the context of manifestation means that as we move towards our goals, we're also being transformed by the journey itself. Acting in alignment shows the universe that we're serious about our intentions and ready to receive what we've requested. By embracing this mindset, we can stay open to learning and evolving as we manifest our desires.

Aligning Actions

Sometimes, the actions we need to take will fall well outside our comfort zone. That's okay! Our growth happens when we step beyond what feels safe and familiar. We need to hold an unwavering trust that each step we take, no matter how small, moves us closer to our goals. Be proactive; do something, including any small action, to move toward your goals. This could be as simple as researching a new career path or showing up at the gym.

The guiding belief of manifestation is that the universe responds to our actions. When we act toward our desires, we open the door for opportunities and synchronicities to come into our lives.

6. Let Go and Trust the Process

One of the hardest parts of manifestation is trusting that outcomes will unfold in the exact way they're meant to. I was introduced to this concept when I was working as a traveling leadership consultant for the Sigma Kappa Foundation. As part of my contract, I signed up to travel wherever I was needed, whenever that may be. I wasn't given a schedule and had no control of where I would go. I was traveling across the country leading leadership workshops, and every three to four days I would be sent to a different college campus. I didn't know what my living accommodations would be ahead of my travel or who I was meeting. As part of my training, they emphasized the importance of "trusting the process," that I needed to have faith that there was a reason why they were sending me where they were sending me. As an absolute control freak and hyper planner, that was very hard for me to do, but it forced me to surrender and provide space for the puzzle pieces to align.

Letting go of control is hard, but this experience changed my perception around the concept of control. In life there are things that are in our control and then there are the "uncontrollables." My actions, attitude, energy, how much effort I give, and how I trust people are all within my control. Other peoples' actions, opinions, reactions, happiness—on the other hand—are not within my control. So instead of focusing on trying to control everything and dictate the outcome, I allow life to take its course while I focus on what's in my control: my response, perspective, and reaction to whatever life does in fact throw at me.

MASTERING INTENTIONS

Controllables	Uncontrollables
Your Attitude: How you approach situations and respond to challenges.	**Other Peoples' Actions:** How others behave or treat you.
Your Actions: The decisions you make and how you follow through.	**The Past:** What has already happened and cannot be changed.
Your Effort: How much energy and dedication you put into things.	**External Events:** Natural disasters, accidents, or economic changes.
Your Reactions: How you handle stress, success, and setbacks.	**Timing:** When opportunities or challenges arise.
Your Habits: The routines and practices you adopt in daily life.	**Other Peoples' Opinions:** How others perceive you or your actions.
Your Thoughts: The mindset and beliefs you choose to cultivate.	**Outcomes:** The final result of situations, despite your best efforts.
Your Goals: What you aim for and the steps you take to achieve them.	**Aging:** The natural progression of time and its effects on the body.
Your Boundaries: The limits you set in relationships and environments.	**Genetics:** Inherited traits and predispositions.
Your Time Management: How you prioritize and structure your day.	**Unexpected Challenges:** Sudden obstacles or detours in your plans.
Your Health Choices: Exercise, diet, and sleep habits.	**Environmental Factors:** Weather, traffic, or other situational influences.

Trusting the process is important because you can't control the timing of your manifestations; they'll happen when you're ready to receive them. This is why you must allow the universe to work its magic while you continue to show up and believe in yourself, and one day, those manifestations will start to come to life.

Aligning Actions

Letting go can be challenging—especially if you're used to being in control—but it's an essential part of the manifestation process because it allows you to release resistance and align with the natural flow of the universe. Practice surrendering your desires to the universe and being open to whatever comes. We create space for opportunities when we trust that our desires will manifest in the right way and at the right time. This doesn't mean we give up on our goals; it means we're willing to trust that the universe has a plan that might be even better for us than we imagined.

But before you're able to take this step of letting go and trusting the process, you have to be ready and trained. The process will show you that you can't be a functional camper in the woods if you haven't mastered some basic camping skills. The first thing you have to do is trust yourself. By building out the earlier competencies discussed in this book, you'll build trust in yourself and know that you can navigate any situation.

7. Journal Regularly

Journaling is a great way to explore our thoughts and feelings about manifestation. By forcing yourself to write down your goals, desires, and feelings, you become clear on your words and intentions. It's a more powerful form of expression than simply visualizing because it requires intense articulation, which demands introspection and reflection. When you journal your thoughts and aspirations, you give them tangible form, transforming abstract ideas into clear actionable desires—and we've already established that clarity is the key component to effective manifestation. That's because clarity enables you to understand exactly what you want to attract in your life. Through the repeated act of journaling and recording your thoughts, feelings, and progress, you can track personal growth and notice patterns in your mindset that may need adjustment. Journaling will also further help you visualize and create a connection between your thoughts, words, and emotions. By creating this emotional alignment, you're reinforcing your manifestation and connecting each of the components in the body—your heart, mind, and physical being—required to turn a manifestation into reality.

Aligning Actions

One effective journaling practice is to write as if our desires have already manifested. Describe your life in detail, including how you feel and what you're doing. This not only helps to solidify our vision, but also brings up any doubts or fears you might need to address. Journaling regularly doesn't only keep us connected to our goals, it also makes us aware of our inner dialogue. We're able to explore what's happening in our brains—including what we're thinking and how we're feeling—and how we convey and communicate those thoughts and feelings through words.

A particularly powerful journaling technique is to write down any limiting beliefs or fears you have during your manifestation journey. By bringing these thoughts to the surface, you can work on transforming them into more empowering beliefs. For example, if we notice a fear of failure, we can journal where that fear comes from and how we could reframe it into a belief supporting our success. Journaling allows us to process our emotions and gain clarity, making it an invaluable tool in our manifestation practice.

8. Vision Board

A vision board is a creative, motivating way to visually represent our goals and dreams. The process of creating a vision board engages your creativity and intuition, making the manifestation process more tangible and enjoyable. This consistent focus helps to strengthen your belief in your ability to manifest your desires and keeps you motivated to take action.

Vision boarding works because different people have different ways of identifying goals and visualizing what they want. Through a vision board and objects that you're looking at—things you want to possess, own, or attract—you start to see them out in the world. Whereas before you may have had a blind eye to when they were passing you by, but now that you've put it up on a board and are looking at it daily, you start to realize the opportunity, potential, and possibility that exists all around you. It's similar to the concept of when you say you want to own a certain car. Once you say that out loud, you keep seeing that same car all over the road. Once you identify what you're looking for, you'll start to see it all around you. And when you begin to see it, you'll be ready to take advantage of the opportunity or put yourself in a position where you can get hold of or grab onto it. Personally, vision boards help me filter my feelings for what I might be holding internally, forcing me to use an image to convey the desire and helping me recognize my choices so that I can better filter my attention.

A vision board is more than just a collection of images—it's a powerful tool that helps you focus your energy and attention on what you want to manifest. When you look at your vision board, you're reminded of your goals and the life you're creating.

Aligning Actions

Collect images, words, and symbols from old magazines that resonate with your desires and arrange them on a board where you can see them daily. This visual reminder keeps your goals at the forefront of your mind and helps to reinforce your intentions.

9. Act "As If"

Similar to what we did during our visualization practice, one of the most powerful ways to manifest your desires is to start *acting* as if you already have what you want. This doesn't mean pretending or being fake—it's about embodying the energy and mindset of your desired reality. If you wish to manifest confidence, start behaving like a confident person would. If you want to attract abundance, adopt the habits and attitudes of someone who feels financially secure. By aligning your actions with your desires, you become a match for what you want, and it becomes easier for those things to enter your life.

People often say "fake it till you make it," but something about this never sat right with me. I never want to feel like I'm faking it through life, waiting for something to happen—it feels inauthentic and inactive. I want to feel in motion, empowered, so I've adopted an act "as if" mentality: it's acting as if you're already the person you want to be. In your mind, in your body, you're behaving as the person you're aspiring to be. This way, when you actually become that person, you can start to move into the journey and embrace the transition of power gracefully so that the starkness of change doesn't feel so intense.

In the corporate world, there's an adage that you dress for the job you want, not for the job you have. The flip side of that is that frequently, promotion decisions are made not based on who could be a great candidate to be a senior manager, but who's already acting as if they're a senior manager. In this case, if you're acting as if you already have what you want, the promotion will simply cement the way you've been acting. What human resource professionals find is that just because they promote someone to a new level doesn't mean that person is going to start acting differently. That's why it's a much easier and safer decision to give the job to the person who's already been acting as if they have the role, as well as the title, respect, and authority that comes along with it.

Aligning Actions

Acting "as if" helps to bridge the gap between our current reality and our desired reality. It's a way of signaling to the universe and to ourselves that we're ready to receive what we want. This practice can also help us overcome limiting beliefs by giving us a taste of what it feels like to live our dream life. Over time, these small changes in behavior and mindset will align our energy with our desires, making manifestation feel more natural and effortless.

Exercise 6.2: "Future casting"

Once you have a certain comfort level with your manifestation practice, you can take your manifestations one step further by "future casting." Jesse Itzler is an American entrepreneur, author, and rapper. He is the co-founder of Marquis Jet, one of the largest private jet card companies in the world, a partner in Zico Coconut Water, the founder of The 100 Mile Group and one of the owners of the NBA's Atlanta Hawks. When he was interviewed on the Rich Roll Podcast,[38] he encouraged people to think in moments, not years, and to then think backwards from those moments to create urgency for how we prioritize our time and make decisions around it. He asked host Rich how old his parents were and how often he saw them, to which Rich responded seventy-six and seventy-four, and twice a year, respectively. Jesse then challenged listeners by pointing out that if Rich's parents only had five years left to live, that would mean Rich would only see them ten more times. He concluded by asking the audience to contemplate: how does that change how you would plan and spend your time? How does that shift priorities? This was a powerful framing and a compelling example of the practice of future casting.

Future casting is anticipating future life moments, achievements, and struggles, and forecasting when or if they'll happen in the future. But it's also about how you'll act accordingly: how you'll act differently today knowing these things will happen in the future. Future casting helps you anticipate and intentionally

---

[38] Rich Roll, "Jesse Itzler: Tackling Life Plateaus & Getting Comfortable Being Uncomfortable | Rich Roll Podcast," hosted by Rich Roll, podcast, posted by Rich Roll, August 4, 2022, YouTube, https://www.youtube.com/watch?v=nHJMVSmoY3c.

shape your path ahead. By tapping into the feelings and energy behind manifestation, you can use future casting to align your thoughts, emotions, and actions.

Often, our mental state is disrupted because we have unexpected obstacles, challenges, losses, and hardships in life that starts to shatter us. It derails us from what we're planning, the intention we set, and where we want to go. By future casting, you're able to have an honest conversation with yourself about the various milestones and hardships you can anticipate throughout your life. These could be experiencing loss, losing a job, getting promoted, having a baby, or getting married, for example. This isn't holistic and there will always be other unexpected things that come up, however, when you start to look at the experiences you'll have over a longer period of time, you can start to think about how your life and how you as a person will change because of them. You can start to shift your thinking to what you can do now to make sure you're prepared for when something comes and what you can do to ensure you don't look back and say you weren't ready or feel regret. That's what future casting is: removing yourself out of the day-to-day visualization and manifestation practices and forecasting your life years down the road.

In the corporate world, the ability and responsibility for future casting is the difference between a board, CEO, vice president, director, and manager. Boards of directors look at five year horizons of time, CEOs are asked to plan for three years, vice presidents are planning for a year at a time, and directors operate on a quarter-to-quarter basis. Managers are operating on month-to-month, week-to-week or even day-to-day basis.

The ability to think in terms of long-term horizons in the corporate world distinguishes executives in terms of respect, capability, and influence. This principle can be applied to our personal lives, where we essentially serve as both the CEO and board of directors of our own journey. It's crucial to think beyond the immediate day-to-day and consider our vision for the next three to five years.

If we focus solely on daily operations, we're essentially functioning as an hourly employee—reactive and task-driven, like an entry-level worker being directed on what to do and when. To break free from this mindset, we must first master our day-to-day responsibilities, then elevate ourselves to the strategic level, where we can plan and execute with a long-term perspective. This shift is key to leading our lives with purpose and achieving sustainable growth.

Personally, I plan to have a significant other in my life, which leads me to ask: how could that change my career trajectory? I know I will eventually lose my grandparents and parents; how does that change how I spend my time, effort, energy, and communication with my parents and grandparents today so that I can be more prepared for when that happens in the future?

Future casting helps you identify contingency plans, actions, or reactions so you're not ambushed by unfolding events. Here's how you can start:

1) Place yourself in a situation.
2) Identify the outcomes of that situation.
3) Reflect on the feelings associated with the outcome.
4) Plan how you will change your behavior or your decision making to take control and shift your feelings associated with the outcome.

A friend of mine was contemplating putting their house on the market, but were overwhelmed by how they might potentially regret that decision. Instead of acting abruptly, they decided to ease into the situation; they tested the waters. To see how they would feel about leaving their home—a property where they'd built their life, enjoyed endless memories, and spent many great years in—they decided to rent it before committing to sell. This was their contingency plan; they made a slow transition to help them before taking the big leap. They would be able to understand their real feelings rather than *anticipating* how they would feel. They placed themselves either by proxy or by scenario into the situation and unpacked the resulting feelings. Ultimately, this helped them make an informed decision, and they realized they weren't attached to the home itself, but rather the time spent there. After looking at how their life had shifted and changed, they were comfortable moving onto the next practice and were ready to say goodbye to their lifelong home.

Another friend and I were talking about preparing for death and loss—something we'll all experience in life, but so often don't prepare for. He shared that as his father was getting older and becoming sicker, he and his wife made the decision to take some time off work—uninterrupted time—to ask all of the questions they felt went unanswered. To learn about his childhood, to hear his memories, and to listen to his stories. They gave him the stage to share, talk, and rejoice in all of the incredible moments that made him who he was. When his father passed, this experience didn't make the loss any less powerful—he'll always yearn for more time, answers, memories, and laughs—but he was able to give himself peace in knowing he had done what was in his power to not experience the feeling of regret.

Oftentimes we feel panic, regret, or remorse because we're surprised by the events that happen in our lives. While there will always remain an element of surprise, there are many events that *will* happen—we just don't know when: when a baby will arrive, when we'll lose a job, when we'll experience heartbreak, and when we'll get the promotion. All of these events can be future casted. You can put yourself in that point in time, experience the feeling as you would with manifestation, and change your behavior today to be prepared for the future.

We can do this in our business, too: when we'll win the big project, when we'll land the next client, when the market will turn, when our business will experience financial hardship, and when a competitor will come in and challenge our existing business model.

Summary of Practice 6: Manifest Your Future

The idea of manifestation might feel overwhelming or even a little "out there" at first. But I can tell you from experience that amazing things can happen when we commit to these practices and genuinely believe in our ability to create our own reality. It's not always a straight path and there will be challenges along the way, but the rewards are worth it. I'm deeply convinced that, with the right mindset and practices, you can achieve anything that you set your mind to.

There are transformative powers in manifestation. Manifestation is the process of bringing your desires into reality through intention, belief, and aligned action. By focusing on the law of attraction, the power of belief, and the process of becoming, you learn to create your future with clarity and purpose.

Manifestation isn't just about thinking positively; it's about deeply feeling the emotions behind your desires and visualizing yourself in the life you want to create. Through daily practices like setting intentions, visualizing, making affirmations, and practicing gratitude, you align your energy with your goals. When you begin to trust the process, believe in yourself, and understand that everything you manifest will come to fruition in the right time, manifestation can be used as an empowering tool that can help you shape the life and future you desire.

Implications for Innerwork

- Use manifestation to align your thoughts, beliefs, and actions with your aspirations.
- Cultivate patience and faith in the unfolding of your journey, letting go of the need to control every detail.
- Begin each day with clear, positive intentions to shape your mindset and guide your actions.
- Regularly acknowledge the positives in your life, shifting focus from "lack" to "abundance."
- Maintain unwavering belief in your ability to manifest your goals.
- Embody the mindset and behaviors of your desired future self.

Implications for Teamship

- Communicate frequently to align team members with a collective vision for a shared future.
- Cultivate a team-wide practice of gratitude.
- Ensure everyone is working towards a shared outcome with clear intentions.
- Engage in future casting as a team to anticipate potential challenges and opportunities.
- Promote visualization to help team members see and feel the success they're working toward.
- Build a team culture that trusts in the collective process, allowing space for the team to adapt and grow together while navigating the journey toward their goals.

Practice 7

CREATE EMPOWERING HABITS

Become obsessed—obsessed with the person you need to become in order to live the life you want to live.

Society has us convinced—has us programmed—to believe that obsession is a bad thing, that it's unhealthy. We're taught to believe that you can't control your obsessions, but that your obsessions will control you. I disagree with this. I believe that mindful obsessions are the greatest driving force for success. There's no question that the best entrepreneurs, athletes, and artists are all obsessed with their craft. They're obsessed with the process, training, work, details, journey, and with self-improvement.

Obsession requires intense focus and unwavering dedication. The obsessed don't shy away from failure. In fact, they recognize how crucial failure is as part of the process and keep forging forward anyway.

Take Michael Jordan: his competitive drive and obsession with winning made him one of the greatest basketball players

MASTERING INTENTIONS

in history. In his famous 1997 Nike ad he said, "I've missed more than nine thousand shots in my career. I've lost almost three hundred games. Twenty-six times I've been trusted to take the game-winning shot and missed. I've failed over and over and over again in my life. And that is why I succeed."[39] He was known for pushing himself and his teammates relentlessly, leading by example, and pushing everyone to strive for constant improvement.

Or take Taylor Swift: she's one of the most influential figures in music history and one of the greatest performers of all time. She said, "Fearless is getting back up and fighting for what you want over and over again ... even though every time you've tried before you've lost."[40]

Throughout her career, Taylor Swift has been able to reinvent herself with each new album she releases while still keeping her artistic integrity and personal connection with her audience intact.

Dr. Seuss's obsession with creativity and storytelling has made him a timeless author that has influenced generations of children. He said, "The more that you read, the more things you will know. The more that you learn, the more places you'll go."[41]

Later in life, I was surprised to learn that while an undergraduate at Dartmouth College, Theodor Seuss Geisel adopted

---

[39] "Failure," advertisement, featuring Michael Jordan, created by Nike, 1997, reuploaded by JayMJ23, YouTube, August 25, 2006, https://www.youtube.com/watch?v=45mMioJ5szc.

[40] Larry Kim. "These 7 Quotes From Taylor Swift Will Make You Work Your Ass Off." *Inc.* n.d. Accessed January 8, 2025. https://www.inc.com/larry-kim/these-7-quotes-from-taylor-swift-will-make-you-work-your-ass-off.html.

[41] Dr. Seuss, *I Can Read with My Eyes Shut!* (New York: Random House, 1978).

the pen name Dr. Seuss. Seuss was the maiden name of his mother and he added Dr. because his father had always wanted him to practice medicine, and he manifested that pen name into one of the most recognized in the world!

Oprah Winfrey's work has inspired millions of people around the world. As a media mogul, her commitment to personal growth and self-improvement translates on- and off-screen. She said, "Create the highest, grandest vision possible for your life because you become what you believe."[42]

Steve Jobs revolutionized the way we interact with technology, creating products that seamlessly blend innovation and design. He famously said, "Your work is going to fill a large part of your life, and the only way to be truly satisfied is to do what you believe is great work. And the only way to do great work is to love what you do. If you haven't found it yet, keep looking. Don't settle. As with all matters of the heart, you'll know when you find it. And, like any great relationship, it just gets better and better as the years roll on. So keep looking until you find it. Don't settle."[43]

Sara Blakely, founder of Spanx, took a single idea and a $5,000 investment and has become a billionaire entrepreneur. Involved in every single detail of product design, material selection, and the manufacturing process, she said, "Don't be intimidated by what you don't know. That can be your greatest

---

[42] CO— by U.S. Chamber of Commerce. "Inspirational Oprah Winfrey Quotes to Motivate Your Success." U.S. Chamber of Commerce. n.d. Accessed January 8, 2025. https://www.uschamber.com/co/start/strategy/inspirational-oprah-winfrey-quotes.

[43] Business Insider. "14 Most Inspiring Steve Jobs Quotes." *Inc.* n.d. Accessed January 8, 2025. https://www.inc.com/business-insider/14-most-inspiring-steve-jobs-quotes.html.

strength and ensure that you do things differently from everyone else."[44]

Helen Keller contracted a childhood illness that left her deaf and blind, yet her pursuit to communicate and her obsession for advocacy and education led her to become the first deaf-blind person to earn a Bachelor of Arts and become one of the most impactful spokespeople and policy impactors for people with disabilities. She stated, "Character cannot be developed in ease and quiet. Only through experience of trial and suffering can the soul be strengthened, ambition inspired, and success achieved."[45]

Think of other greats: Tom Brady, Elon Musk, Jeff Bezos, Kobe Bryant, Pablo Picasso, and Serena Williams, to name a few, and each one is obsessed. Obsession, when channeled positively, can be a powerful driver of success, enabling individuals to push beyond conventional limits and achieve extraordinary accomplishments.

It's important to note that there's a price to obsession. Obsession is a fixation; it's intense and it can be selfish. Obsession never turns off. In the same vein, greatness is a fixation: it's intense, it can be selfish, and—in order to achieve it—it means never turning off. So how do you become obsessed if you haven't yet identified your passion? And how do you turn that obsession into greatness?

---

[44] Entrepreneur. "9 Inspiring Quotes from Self-Made Billionaire and Spanx Founder Sara Blakely." https://www.entrepreneur.com/leadership/9-inspiring-quotes-from-self-made-billionaire-and-spanx/319539?utm_source=chatgpt.com. n.d. Accessed January 8, 2025.

[45] Goodreads. "Helen Keller Quotes." https://www.goodreads.com/author/quotes/7275.Helen_Keller?utm_source=chatgpt.com. n.d. Accessed January 8, 2025.

For me, I've been able to simplify it by becoming obsessed with my life journey, how I want to live my life, and why I love it. I boil it down to becoming obsessed with the habits and behaviors I need to possess in order to be the person I hope to one day become. That's where it starts.

Obsession has allowed me to hyper focus on my habits and behaviors. It's forced me to create disciplines in my life, the building blocks that help me work towards building the structure required in order to be the person I want to be in the future. My disciplines and behaviors are not for the person I am today, they're for the woman I intend to become.

The Multiplier Effect of Empowering Habits

Discipline, routine, consistency and accountability are foundational for creating empowering habits. While intertwined concepts, they each have distinct roles and functions in the journey of becoming obsessed.

Discipline is a choice. It's the ability to control one's behavior, emotions, and impulses to stay focused on goals and tasks, even when it's difficult. Discipline is the force that pushes you to take action, especially when you aren't motivated. It helps you make decisions that align with your goals, even when distractions or temptations arise. A simple example is choosing to work on a project instead of watching TV because you know it's important for your progress. A disciplined practice that I've implemented is reviewing my monthly financial forecasting and budgeting. The last Sunday of every month, I time block my day for financial planning, reviewing personal income and expenses as well as business income and expenses for the past thirty days, and studying the feasibility of various business ventures and projects. By setting aside this time every month, I'm able to stay current and focused to ensure I stay on track—and if I'm not—recalibrate where needed.

Routine is a set of habits or activities that you regularly follow in a specific order, often at particular times. Routine provides structure and predictability, making it easier to manage time and energy. It reduces the need to constantly make decisions about what to do next, as actions become automatic. An example is your daily routines. One daily routine could be waking up at 8:00 a.m. and scrolling on social media for an hour. Yet another, the disciplined routine, could include waking up at 6:00 a.m., meditating, and then starting your workday. We all have routines every single day, but the discipline to make your routines serve you is what separates productive routines from unproductive ones. My typical morning routine includes waking up early, practicing my positive self-talk and gratitude affirmations in the mirror, working out, and being the first one in the office. When I execute on this every day, I set myself up for success.

Consistency is the practice of regularly repeating an action over time, maintaining a steady pattern of behavior. Consistency ensures that the actions you take daily add up over time, leading to significant progress and results. It's the key to long-term success. Consistency is my favorite part of the equation because when you add up routine and discipline and multiply it by consistency, you experience the multiplier effect. Looking at the two disciplines and routines mentioned above, by practicing positive self-talk, gratitude, and working out every day and implementing monthly financial check-ins, I'm physically, mentally, and fiscally my healthiest self. If I just did this for one month, I would feel good. After doing this for a year, I would feel strong and empowered. By doing these routines and disciplines for years, I feel unstoppable.

Accountability is the obligation to take responsibility for your actions and to be answerable to others (or yourself) for your performance and progress. Accountability helps you stay committed to your goals by creating a system of checks and balances. It can come from external sources, like mentors, peers, or accountability partners, or from internal self-monitoring. If you don't hold yourself accountable for your disciplines, routines, and the consistency of your behavior, you won't experience the results you're striving for. So, share your goals with a friend who checks in on your progress regularly, or use a journal to track and reflect on your daily actions. Accountability is the glue that holds discipline, routine, and consistency together. Personally, I find accountability to be the hardest piece of the puzzle—that's why I've enlisted various partners and measures to ensure I stay accountable. For example, my friends, family, and work colleagues help me stay accountable for my healthy life choices, my business partners hold me accountable for my business disciplines, and my accountant and financial planner hold me accountable so I stay on track with my financial planning goals.

Let's simplify and put these concepts into practice. Most of us would agree that we aspire to improve our physical health. So, let's use that as an example:

1) **You decide to get fit.** Discipline initiates the journey by helping you make decisions that align with your goals, even when it's challenging.
2) **You create a workout plan that fits into your daily schedule.** Routine creates a predictable structure that makes disciplined actions easier to maintain over time.

3) **You commit to exercising at the same time every day.** Consistency ensures that these disciplined actions, when repeated regularly as part of a routine, lead to long-term progress.
4) **You tell a friend about your goal, and they agree to check in with you weekly to see how you're doing.** Accountability reinforces all these elements by providing motivation and feedback, ensuring you stay on track. Knowing that someone else (or even your future self) will review your progress can increase your commitment and adherence to your routine.

The Multiplier Effect = (Routine + Discipline) x Consistency x Accountability

The multiplier effect is when the positive habits you have now pay off for the rest of your life. Similarly, bad habits you have now can hurt you for the rest of your life. One or two bad habits in your forties or fifties can cost you five years in your seventies. Just think about smoking cigarettes, consuming too much sugar, or not exercising. There's no doubt these habits would impact your health in the future, but what about not exercising your brain? What would happen if you stopped reading or problem solving daily? What would happen to your financial health if you stopped saving, budgeting, or setting money aside for a rainy day? Changing those habits now can work to give you time back. If you consistently dedicate thirty minutes every day to learning a new language, for example, over time you'll become fluent in that language. If you consistently dedicate time every day to work out, eventually you'll have the physical health you aspire to have. If you put money into a retirement account every year, one day you'll have the financial flexibility and freedom to make different choices as you age.

Now let's bring the multiplier effect into a business example. When I started my company, I knew I wanted to create something different, something special, but the competition was fierce. According to the National Association of REALTORS (NAR), there are over 1.5 million members in the United States real estate profession.[46] In the world, there are an estimated four to six million.[47] I'm certainly not smarter than all of them, so what could I do to stand out? To make me different? The answer to the question was work ethic. If there was one thing in my control, I could outwork everyone in order to become the best. That's where obsession comes in.

Using the same method as above, but incorporating my goal of out-performing everyone:

- I decided to work harder and smarter—Discipline.
- I developed systems and strategies to optimize my time and performance—Routine.
- I commit to being the first one in and last one out every single day—Consistency.
- I write down my goals and review them weekly to hold myself accountable. I share my goals and routines with my colleagues, friends, and family so they hold me accountable, too. I share my routine and disciplines on

---

[46] "History," National Association of REALTORS, accessed August 15, 2024, https://www.nar.realtor/about-nar/history.

[47] National Association of REALTORS®. "How Many Real Estate Professionals Exist Worldwide?" *nar.realtor*. Accessed January 8, 2025. https://www.nar.realtor/global/how-many-real-estate-professionals-exist-worldwide.

my social media platforms so my audience also holds me accountable—Accountability.

While I'm simplifying this, don't get me wrong—discipline, routine, consistency, and accountability aren't easy. I would say mastering them is harder than the task itself. It's harder than finding a job, becoming skilled in a profession, and even making money. However, mastering these skills is where the growth happens. You can find the job, become skilled, and make money, but how do you take it to the next level? This is how. This is mastering intentions.

When I think about my routines and habits, I start by thinking about what I need to do daily, weekly, monthly, quarterly, and annually. Then I think macro: what are the big things I need to accomplish in order to have the compounding effect I desire? For example:

- Every day, I need to take care of my mind and body.
- Every week, I need to check in with my companions: family, friends, and employees.
- Every month, I need to make sure our sales benchmarks are on track.
- Every quarter, I need to evaluate growth and progression and address bottlenecks that arise.
- Every year, I need to review last year's performance and set goals for the upcoming year.

Now that I know my big picture objectives, how do I build out the routines, consistency and accountability practices to support them?

Systems are the root of consistency.

Best-selling author, Jim Collins, says it perfectly. "The best companies never transform to greatness in 'one fell swoop'. There is no single defining action, no grand program, no one killer innovation, no solitary lucky break, no miracle moment. Sustainable transformations [to greatness] follow a predictable pattern of build-up and breakthrough. Like pushing on a giant heavy flywheel, it takes a lot of effort to get the thing moving at all, but with persistent pushing in a consistent direction over a long period of time, the flywheel builds momentum, eventually hitting a point of breakthrough."[48]

To support my discipline of taking care of my mind and my body—I hold myself accountable to a series of consistent routines. I refer to these as my systems—I build a routine by time blocking every day. My time block and my calendar absolutely run my life; it's how I stay on task, organized, and keeps me focused.

Time blocking is my singular most impactful system that enhances my ability to lead, delegate, and manage. As entrepreneur, author, and motivational speaker Jim Rohn put it, "Either you run the day, or the day runs you."[49]

Other systems that I rely on are System Sundays, Inbox Zero, Financial Mapping and the Mastery Journal, which I'll elaborate on below. Following the structure for each system as detailed exercises below, enables you to create new efficiencies for your life and business.

---

[48] Jim Collins. *Good to Great: Why Some Companies Make the Leap...and Others Don't*. New York: HarperBusiness, 2001.

[49] "Jim Rohn - Either you run the day or the day runs you." Jim Rohn, BrainyQuote, accessed August 15, 2024, https://www.brainyquote.com/quotes/jim_rohn_162051.

Exercise 7.1: Time Blocking

Time blocking is a powerful productivity routine where you schedule specific blocks of time for particular tasks or activities. This method helps you manage your day more effectively, reduce distractions, and ensure that you allocate sufficient time to your most important tasks.

Step 1: Identify Your Goals and Priorities

Start by identifying your key goals and priorities. Never-ending to-do lists can be overwhelming and exhausting. While keeping a running to-do list is important as to not forget tasks, the mistake people make far too often is moving down a to-do list chronologically or identifying the easiest tasks first, accomplishing those, and then procrastinating on the more challenging tasks—which are often the most important tasks that require the more immediate attention.

Step 2: Identify Nonnegotiables

Once you have your list of priorities, start by starring your nonnegotiables. My nonnegotiables are the tasks that absolutely must be done by the end of the day; I don't allow myself to go home, leave the office, or turn off my computer until they're completed. If they're done by 3:00 p.m., great. If it takes me until 1:00 a.m., then I stay put until 1:00 a.m. to ensure they're completed. This is a promise I make to myself; this is my disciplined practice that holds me accountable for doing what I say I'm going to do in the time I promised myself I would do it.

Step 3: Time Block Previously Scheduled Tasks

On a piece of paper, organize your day into time blocks from the moment you wake up until you go to bed. The first blocks I write down are the scheduled activities I've already committed myself to: 5:30 a.m. wake up, 6:30–7:30 a.m. workout, my shower that follows, and any other calls or meetings that I have planned for the day. Then I block the times in between what's already committed to. If I know I'll be seated at my desk by 8:30 a.m. but my first call isn't until 10:00 a.m., then I have one and a half hours of a block which I can keep as is, or parse into a smaller chunk of time and allocate more activities to. I'll take the first thirty minutes of that and leave it as a placeholder for delegating tasks. This is when you can refer back to the list: how many nonnegotiables are there? Start by scheduling nonnegotiables first before the day gets busy. After you've scheduled your nonnegotiables, cross them off your original to-do list and see what remains.

Step 4: Delegate Tasks
(Tasks Involving Other People)

The next items I look at on the list are what tasks I can delegate, or which tasks require other people's involvement or collaboration. Being that these involve others, it requires a bit more coordination. The thirty minutes that I block at the top of every day are for, first, sending emails to my team with delegated tasks, responsibilities, and objectives, and, second, scheduling/coordinating time blocked activities with others that fall later in the day. By delegating early in the morning, before the workday starts for the rest of my team, I ensure that this email is one of the first in their inbox and helps them prioritize their days. After you've scheduled your tasks involving others, cross them off your original to-do list and see what remains.

Step 5: Fill In the Rest of the Day

Moving down your list, continue thinking with priority at the forefront. Not only where your priorities are, but what is the highest and best use of your time during the day. Calls, follow-up, and work objectives are great midday tasks, whereas solo activities like creative thinking, big picture planning, and longer-term planning I save for my after-hours time blocks because they don't require turnaround or involvement from anyone else.

Step 6: Review and Adjust

At the end of every day, I evaluate my day's performance in relation to staying on track. Did I miss something? Did something take longer than expected? Was I able to get ahead because I overestimated how much time an activity would take?

Example of a Daily Time Blocking Schedule

Time	Activity	Description
8:00 a.m. - 8:30 a.m.	Morning Routine	Breakfast, exercise, and preparation for the day.
8:30 a.m. - 9:00 a.m.	Planning and Prioritization	Review goals, plan the day's tasks.
9:00 a.m. - 11:00 a.m.	Project Work	Focused time on key project tasks.
11:00 a.m. - 11:30 a.m.	Email and Correspondence	Respond to emails and messages.
11:30 a.m. - 12:00 p.m.	Meetings	Attend scheduled meetings.
12:00 p.m. - 1:00 p.m.	Lunch Break	Rest and have lunch.
1:00 p.m. - 3:00 p.m.	Creative Work	Time for brainstorming and creative tasks.
3:00 p.m. - 3:30 p.m.	Short Break	Quick break to recharge.
3:30 p.m. - 5:00 p.m.	Administrative Tasks	Handle paperwork, reports, and other administrative duties.
5:00 p.m. - 5:30 p.m.	Review and Planning	Review the day's work, plan for tomorrow.
5:30 p.m. - 6:00 p.m.	Wrap-Up and Wind Down	Finalize any loose ends and prepare for the end of the day.
6:00 p.m. onward	Personal Time	Family, relaxation, hobbies.

Time is the biggest limiting factor in life. We can't get more of it, so being diligent about how and where we spend it is absolutely crucial. The best way I've been able to figure out how to best control time is through effective time management via time blocking. It helps me optimize productivity and stay on track to achieve my goals. By prioritizing tasks, managing deadlines, and scheduling work and my personal life, time blocking has helped me reduce stress, improve decision-making, and ensure steady progress. Overall, mastering time management leads to greater efficiency, better quality work, reduced stress, and a healthier life.

In addition to daily time blocking, another daily habit that I employ is positive self-talk, which I discussed earlier in this book. While I practice positive self-talk every single morning, I also default to it many times throughout the day through programmed muscle memory. This has become an exercise that helps tremendously with discipline because when I feel myself veering in the wrong direction, I can often use positive self-talk to get me back on track.

Exercise 7.2: System Sundays

After you master the day to day, you can start to think about how you can create empowering habits to help you optimize your week. About a year ago, I implemented a new practice into my business called System Sundays which has been a game changer for my company's long-term growth strategy. I chose Sunday as my day for this practice because this is a solo practice that requires my full, undivided attention without interruption from other business activities. It also allows me to get my headspace into an efficient planning mode week after week, ensuring I start the week off strong.

This also means that on Mondays, I can go to my leadership team and explain the new system that I've optimized and built out—because at the heart of this practice is a focus on systemizing life and business. Why? Because systems are fundamental to business success, streamlining operations, and driving efficiency. They ensure consistency, reduce errors, and free up time for strategic growth. Tom Peters, author of *In Search of Excellence*, reinforces this by saying, "Excellent firms don't believe in excellence—only in constant improvement and constant change,"[50] which is driven by adaptive systems. Systems are crucial for maintaining quality, managing growth, and achieving long-term success in business and in life.

While the word *systems* feels very business centric, there are many ways we can incorporate systems that exist in our personal life as well to streamline decision making and reduce stress. A few small examples of how I've been able to utilize systems in my personal life are:

- Each weekend, I identify my outfits for the entire workweek so I don't need to spend time during the week or in the mornings trying to pick out what I'm going to wear for the day. By spending thirty minutes over the weekend on this activity, I can reclaim twenty minutes every single morning. That means instead of spending one hundred hours each week picking out, trying on, and modeling outfits day after day, I can truncate that into thirty minutes in one shot. That means I just added one hour and ten minutes of extra time to my week.
- I also use my weekends as my personal check-in time with friends and family. I work down a list of the companions in my life that I need to check in with; I do this one after another sequentially versus scattered throughout the week. While this may take up more time because conversations with friends and family members can be twenty to thirty minutes instead of a five to ten minute check in at random during the week

---

[50] "Tom Peters - Excellent firms don't believe in excellence - only in constant improvement and constant change." Tom Peters, BrainyQuote, accessed August 17, 2024, https://www.brainyquote.com/quotes/tom_peters_159520.

(or multiple times during the week), I still consider this a more efficient system because I can have completely uninterrupted, focused conversations without distraction or rush. This, in turn, leads to better quality conversations—which is the ultimate goal for my check-in calls.

- Meal prepping is another great personal system; it saves time and helps promote healthier eating habits. By planning and preparing meals in advance, you can streamline grocery shopping, cooking, and portion control, ensuring balanced nutrition throughout the week. This proactive approach minimizes the likelihood of unhealthy food choices and helps manage dietary goals effectively, ultimately leading to improved health and well-being.

In business there are millions of systems we can build, incorporate, and enhance to better optimize our business functions. Each of our systems will vary based on industry, position, and company/team size; however, the process remains the same.

1. Identify

To start, first you must identify and list key areas for improvement. I start by looking at what existing systems, workflows, and routines my company currently has in place. Ideas that can be more universal are email correspondence, prospecting outreach, sales follow-ups, recruiting, hiring and onboarding processes, and marketing initiatives—I list everything. If it's currently a broken system, it doesn't need to stay that way; if it's a system—no matter how long you've been doing it—there's always a way to optimize and enhance it.

After I've identified all of the systems I currently have in place, I start to think of what systems I want to add and where we can increase efficiency. I ask myself: where or what in my process currently doesn't have a system? Because that means we can build one. Nearly everything in business can have a system, and the more you systemize, the more efficient you'll become. Now, I also don't want to overcomplicate the word *systems*, because not every system needs to be complicated or utilize expensive technology. However, all functions of your business can have a documented path and a standard operating procedure for execution which will streamline behaviors as well as help with future planning, training, and the longevity of the function to ensure quality control.

2. Prioritize, Organize, & Schedule

After I have my two lists—the existing systems and the areas for opportunity—I begin prioritizing. Which systems would have the highest impact on my business function and my team's operations? After I set my priority, I physically schedule each of them on each Sunday throughout the course of the year. I then build out a spreadsheet with columns for the date, system name, link to the document file I'm working off of to go back to for ease, and a status column to track progress. Then I schedule to build out each system in my calendar every Sunday as an all-day event. Remember, calendar planning is gold—if it doesn't live there, there's an opportunity I'll forget, become distracted, or not prioritize the function.

3. Break it Down

Week after week, I look at each system and break it down, examining each component of it. I ask myself:

1) How well is my team doing with this system or lack thereof? Are they using the system? If not, why?
2) What support, training, and tools are currently available?
3) Is there a bottleneck in the process?
4) When was the last time I reviewed this system with my employees?
5) What can I do to enhance the system?

If I'm changing a current system, it's important to be able to identify, articulate, and communicate why with my team. Changing a system and then not properly training or communicating the system will have an adverse effect. It's also important to have buy-in with your team when changing systems. Identify the "this is why we're changing this and this is how it will make your life easier, make more money, and improve your productivity."

As I mentioned earlier, not every system needs to become overcomplicated with technology. While technology is certainly a tremendous tool that will enhance efficiency, if you overwhelm your team and employees with exorbitant amounts of tech, they may retreat and not utilize the system at all. Remember this is an ongoing, never-ending process of optimization. Phase One can be a simple checklist or an outlined standard operating procedure (SOP), and Phase Two can be the use of automation tools. If you already have the check list or the SOP, this is where the opportunity for automation can come in and really enhance the efficacy. Automation tools, such as project management software, time-tracking apps, and communication platforms are good areas to start exploring.

4. Establish Routines and Habits

Making systems routine in daily and weekly functions is essential to ensure they're consistently followed. Consistency is king. Regularly following these new processes will reinforce that systems become habitual and second nature.

5. Monitor and Review Performance

Systems are only as good as their effectiveness. Use key performance indicators (KPIs) and other metrics to evaluate the effectiveness of your systems. For business, this might involve productivity metrics; for personal systems, it could include time management efficiency. Each system, depending on the business function and department it's supporting, will have a different KPI. For example, if you're building out all new email response templates to standardize follow-up with clients, a KPI that could be utilized to measure the success of this initiative would be monitoring email response time: did utilizing this template help your team follow up faster than they would have without it? How much time did it save them? How has the consumer response changed due to the new email format? Are you procuring more business because your employees are sharing a more robust and standardized format? These are tangible metrics that have an impact on the bottom line of your organization. I would suggest reviewing newly incorporated systems on a monthly and quarterly basis, making small tweaks as needed, and then, once a year, going through a full optimization of the process to make key, necessary enhancements.

6. Seek Feedback and Iterate

Soliciting feedback from team members, peers, or mentors about the effectiveness of your systems is essential to development and growth. This input can provide valuable insights for improvement. Use feedback and performance data to refine and adjust systems. Optimization is an ongoing process, and systems should evolve to meet changing needs.

7. Foster a Culture of Optimization

Promoting a culture that values continuous improvement and encourages innovative ideas for optimizing processes will make systems collaborative, increase user buy-in, and enhance the efficiency of the system. Providing training and resources to help individuals understand the reasoning and implementation of effective systems and processes will help improve your corporate culture of optimization.

8. Document and Standardize

Documenting systems, processes, and best practices will ensure consistency and will aid in onboarding new team members. Ensure that optimized systems are standardized across the organization or personal routines to maintain uniformity and efficiency.

Exercise 7.3: Inbox Zero

When I ask my team what part of their business function is the most inefficient or creates the most bottlenecks in their workday, I've found the answer to this question more often than not is email management. I can certainly relate, and it took many years of feeling bogged down by my emails, to realize how much managing the organization of my inbox would become a game changer for my time in and out of the office.

Inbox Zero[51] was popularized by Merlin Mann, a productivity expert and blogger. He introduced the concept through his blog and presentations around 2006. Mann, known for his work on personal productivity and time management, developed Inbox Zero as part of his broader productivity system, which emphasizes managing information overload and maintaining a clean, organized workspace.

Mann introduced Inbox Zero as a way to handle email more effectively and avoid the stress of an overflowing inbox. The approach aims to keep one's email inbox empty or close to empty by systematically processing, delegating, or archiving emails. The goal is to ensure that no emails are left unattended and that your inbox serves as a streamlined to-do list. Mann's approach is not just about having an empty inbox, but also about maintaining a manageable system where emails are handled efficiently, reducing stress and increasing productivity. Mann's insights and methods have been influential in how individuals and organizations alike approach email management and productivity.

---

[51] Merlin Mann, "Inbox Zero," Google Tech Talks, July 23, 2007, posted October 8, 2007, by Google TechTalks, YouTube, https://www.youtube.com/watch?v=z9UjeTMb3Yk.

Core Principles

1) **Process Emails Regularly:** Regularly check your email and process messages promptly. This involves categorizing, responding to, delegating, or deleting emails.
2) **Immediate Action:** Address each email with a specific action in mind:
    a) Do It: If it takes less than two minutes, handle it immediately.
    b) Delegate It: If it can be handled by someone else, forward it to the appropriate person.
    c) Defer It: If it requires more time, schedule it for later and move it to a "To-Do" folder.
    d) Delete or Archive It: If it's not relevant or needed, remove it from your inbox.
3) **Organize Efficiently:** Use folders, labels, and filters to organize emails. This helps in managing and retrieving emails effectively without cluttering the inbox.
4) **Set Boundaries:** Allocate specific times during the day to check and process emails, rather than responding impulsively. This helps maintain focus and productivity.

While I've iterated my own version of Inbox Zero, these principles have been the guiding force to help me enhance productivity throughout the day by not allowing my inbox to control my life. Managing your email properly will reduce stress and better allow you to focus on tasks without being distracted by unresolved emails. A more controlled inbox will also allow you to have better organization throughout the day (think back to your time blocking) and will improve response time while preventing important messages from being overlooked.

By implementing Inbox Zero, you can manage your email more effectively, maintain a clear mind, *and* stay on top of important tasks and communications.

Exercise 7.4: Financial Mapping

An intentional life demands clarity of purpose. Two items that highlight purpose clearly are your calendar and your financial apps. As Dave Ramsey wisely said, "A budget is telling your money where to go instead of wondering where it went."[52] By evaluating your spending habits, you can consider whether your financial choices align with your priorities. This exercise is a critical skill that extends far beyond dollars and cents—it's about aligning your financial resources with your values so that your life reflects the things that matter most to you.

Step 1: Ask "If I Had All the Money I Needed, What Would I Do?"

Let's start by taking a moment to think expansively. Imagine, just for a second, that you have all the money you need. What would you do with it? Close your eyes if it helps and reflect for a moment. The key to this exercise isn't in the fantasy of endless riches, but in revealing your core desires. What are the things that genuinely bring you joy? What makes your life feel rich beyond just financial wealth?

---

[52] "Quote by Dave Ramsey: 'John Maxwell says a budget (for your money) is telling your money where to go instead of wondering where it went. Managing time is the same; you will either tell your day what to do or you will wonder where it went.'" Dave Ramsey, Goodreads, accessed August 20, 2024, https://www.goodreads.com/quotes/7145116-john-maxwell-says-a-budget-for-your-money-is-telling.

Write down a paragraph or at least seven bullet points answering that question. Here are a few prompts to help guide you:

- Would you travel more? And if so, where would you go?
- Would you give back to your community or donate to causes close to your heart?
- Would you invest in experiences with family and friends? What kinds of experiences?
- Would you invest more in your education or personal development?
- Would you buy things or experiences? What kind of expenditures would make you feel fulfilled?

These reflections help uncover what truly matters to you. Based on my life experiences, I believe it's not the amount of money that counts, but how we direct that money toward creating a life that reflects our priorities.

Step 2: Conduct a Spending Diagnostic

Start by gathering data on your spending. Wherever you track it—whether through apps or your credit card and bank statements—review your financial activity over the past year (this isn't about judgment; it's about insight). You've had time to dream and imagine, but the reality of aligning your life with your priorities means facing where you are today. With this step, you'll conduct a regular and honest "spending diagnostic."

Here are some key questions to ask as you comb through your spending:

- What did I spend my money on? Break it into housing, food, entertainment, travel, education, and investments.
- What life am I buying with this spending? Look beyond the purchases themselves and think about the experiences and patterns they represent. Are you spending on things that bring you joy, or are you simply going through the motions?
- Is this the life I want? This is the most critical question. It's easy to get stuck in a pattern where our spending doesn't reflect our true desires. Are you investing in your passions, or are you pouring money into things that don't really matter in the grand scheme of your life?

Patterns will emerge, and some may surprise you. Perhaps you spent more on convenience and less on meaningful experiences. Or maybe you've been saving a lot but feel like you're missing out on opportunities to enjoy life right now.

Step 3: Reflect and Adjust

Now comes the moment of truth. Take a few moments to reflect on the following question: *Does my spending pattern move me closer to or further away from a life aligned with my priorities?*

Be honest and concrete in your answer. If you've identified family as a top priority, how much money are you spending on experiences with your loved ones? Do you spend more on individual activities, such as subscriptions, solo hobbies, or personal shopping, than on family experiences like outings, vacations, or dinners together? For example, if one of your priorities is to deepen your connection with your family, but most of your money is spent on things that keep you apart—like excessive solo entertainment or personal luxuries—there's likely a misalignment. It doesn't mean you've failed, but it's a sign of an opportunity for course correction.

Reflecting on your spending is not about guilt; it's about empowerment. It allows you to ask yourself, "What changes can I make and am I willing to make in order to align my money with my priorities better?" Once you can answer that, the path forward becomes much more straightforward.

Step 4: Align Your Money with Your Priorities

Once you've identified your priorities and evaluated your financial situation, it's time to take action. Here are some practical steps you can take to align your spending with your values better:

1) **Create a Values-Based Budget:** Once you've identified what truly matters, create a budget that reflects those values. If family is a priority, allocate some of your income to family-related experiences or investments.
2) **Cut Out the Excess:** Look for areas where you're spending money that doesn't contribute to your core values. This might mean canceling subscriptions you no longer use or cutting back on unnecessary purchases that don't add joy to your life.
3) **Automate Your Priorities:** Use technology to your advantage. Automate savings for what matters, like a family vacation fund, an investment account, or a charity donation. This way, you ensure that your money

is going where it should without you having to think about it.
4) **Invest in Yourself:** If education, personal growth, or health are important to you, invest in them. It's easy to prioritize things that have an immediate payoff, but investing in yourself is one of the best long-term investments you can make.
5) **Plan for the Future, but Don't Forget the Present:** It's easy to get caught up in saving for the future, but life is happening now. Strike a balance between saving for the future and living your life in the present moment. This is where prioritizing experiences, relationships, and personal fulfillment comes into play.
6) **Be Flexible and Reassess Regularly:** Life changes, and so will your priorities. Make it a habit to reassess your budget and spending regularly—at least annually—to ensure they still align with where you want to go.

The Power of Intentional Spending

Ultimately, your financial decisions are about more than just money—they're about designing a life that reflects who you are and what you value. Financial freedom doesn't come from having all the money in the world; it comes from understanding what you truly want and making intentional choices to align your resources with those desires. Even with clear financial mapping and preparedness, managing finances and controlling cash flow is variable and ever changing. There is never one clear, right answer and there will always be unexpected life events and business expenses that will arise. The most important thing when taking a risk—when betting on yourself—is to know that you need to give yourself the grace and time in order to reap the rewards of your sacrifice.

Personally, I spent the entire decade of my twenties stressed out about money. At twenty-two, I took a job making $13,000 a year because I knew I would learn an invaluable amount about myself in the role that would come back tenfold. At twenty-three, I started in real estate and closed out the year making $11,000. At twenty-four, I felt I had no idea what I was doing and took a sidestep from trying to build a sales business into becoming an administrator in the field so I could learn more. I accepted an entry-level administrator salary because I knew I needed tactical training in order to learn. By twenty-five, I realized what was needed in order to start building a sales business and started again. By twenty-six, I lost every dollar I had ever saved—and in turn invested—in a real estate investment that went sideways. At twenty-seven, I started over again, and then again at twenty-nine, when I started my current company. If there was one thing that stayed consistent throughout all of these attempts, it was that I knew I was betting on myself. I knew the financial discomfort I was signing up for and I was prepared to make the personal sacrifices in order to achieve the professional reward.

Financial mapping and preparedness are indispensable for entrepreneurs and young professionals embarking on new business ventures. By creating detailed financial statements, developing budgets and forecasts, and identifying gaps and opportunities, you lay the groundwork for a successful and sustainable business. Regular monitoring and adaptability further ensure that your financial strategies align with your goals and respond to evolving circumstances. Embracing these practices equips you to face the challenges of entrepreneurship with confidence and clarity.

Exercise 7.5: The Mastery Journal

Creating empowering habits can often feel very mechanical, as we oftentimes remove emotion from function in order to create optimization. But in life, emotions drive us, and in business, emotions create culture and connection. This is why it's important to build habits that become emotioncentric, and that's where the Mastery Journal comes in.

The purpose of the Mastery Journal is to align yourself and your companions around the person you're becoming in order to achieve that goal or objective. This journal isn't focused on the end goal, but rather on self-development, self-help, self-growth, and self-awareness in order to enhance your social awareness in relation to others and how you're collaborating and working in conjunction with others.

The Mastery Journal is a very effective tool for personal and professional growth, but it's not a solo sport. Successful people tend to isolate and scaffold their talents and passions to find their personal purpose. They emphasize the need to identify and prioritize personal strengths and reflect on emotions in order to achieve success and happiness in life and work. The Mastery Journal is a tool for working with companions to accomplish better, joint successes. It helps us reflect on the following:

- As a leader, who am I interacting with?
- What was my role in the success of this or where did I add to it?

The Mastery Journal is a new tool that's very different from daily journaling. I use it constantly to realign my intention and activate my team's purpose, amplify our power, and lead with lasting impact. It acts as a source of constant reflection, which is why I use it after any big milestone, setback, or event. The point of the Mastery Journal is to reflect inward on your contributions and emotions in relation to what happened and document it. Questions I covered in recent Mastery Journal entries include:

- What did I do to make me feel accomplished and proud?
- What did I excel at? What will I do differently next time?
- What was seen as valuable to my companions?
- How did my contributions make them feel?
- What did I deliver that was seen as valuable?
- What contribution did I make?
- How did my contribution make me feel?
- How am I as a leader?

My Mastery Journal is episodic, but a routine practice. It forces me to answer the same questions repeatedly about different circumstances in order to push me to be purposeful and build community through programming, execution, delivery, and goals.

Summary of Practice 7: Create Empowering Habits

Empowering habits are the foundation for building a fulfilling and successful life and business. Habits are the silent architects of our future, sculpting our character, shaping our outcomes, and influencing our overall well-being.

By intentionally cultivating habits that align with our values and goals, we empower ourselves to navigate life's challenges with greater resilience and purpose. Each habit, whether it's Time Blocking, System Sundays, Inbox Zero, Financial Mapping, or utilizing the Mastery Journal, serve as building blocks for our personal and professional growth. These routines not only streamline our efforts, but also foster a sense of control and direction.

The journey to developing empowering habits isn't always straightforward. It requires patience, persistence, and self-compassion. There will be setbacks and obstacles, but each is an opportunity for learning and refinement. Embrace the process, celebrate small victories, and remain committed to your path.

The power to transform your life lies in your daily choices and actions. By nurturing habits that inspire and uplift, you lay the groundwork for a future that isn't only successful, but deeply fulfilling.

Implications for Innerwork

- Be obsessed with your habits in order to achieve extraordinary accomplishments.
- Be intentional about how you spend your time.
- Use tools like time blocking to stay focused on what matters most.
- Track your progress through journaling.
- Be consistent: small, deliberate actions taken daily build the foundation for long-term success.
- Cultivate habits that empower you to thrive, both personally and professionally.

- Seek routine, discipline, consistency, and accountability in your habits.

Implications for Teamship

- Help build team habits through clear goals, delegating responsibilities, and creating accountability systems.
- Use tools like team calendars, progress trackers, and regular check-ins to ensure the team stays on course.
- Encourage collaboration and support by fostering habits that build trust and communication within the team.
- As a leader, model empowering habits that emphasize discipline, collaboration, and strategic growth.
- Celebrate milestones and reinforce habits that contribute to long-term team success.

INTENTION THREE

Lead with Lasting Impact

Practice 8

FOSTER TEAMSHIP

Everything becomes more meaningful through experiencing shared success. There's magic in collaboration.

Far too often in my life, I've retreated into isolation as a defense mechanism. When life would get messy, I would close myself off, pulling back and separating myself from friends and family—afraid to ask for help, depend on people, allow myself to become vulnerable, and let people in. When I look back on the darkest times in my life, they weren't because of the life circumstances that were occurring, but because I felt completely alone and isolated during those moments. Even during peaks in my life, when I should have been on top of the world—yet somehow felt hollow inside—it was because I was afraid to let people in to experience the moments of joy with me. But what is life if we're living it alone? What is building and growing and becoming if it becomes a solo sport? It becomes merely a game, not a journey.

When I recognized this, I started thinking about the best times in my life, the happiest moments. Those times weren't the best because of achieving a milestone, receiving an award, or having a certain amount of money in my bank account. They were the times my family was happiest, my friendships were the strongest, and my team was in alignment. Those best moments were rooted in people—not achievements.

People define experiences. People shape lives. People change the world. People are the essence of a team, and Teamship is a way of life.

Teamship is the art of creating and nurturing a collective where individuals align their strengths, efforts, and goals to achieve a shared vision. It's more than teamwork—it's a philosophy rooted in unity, mutual respect, and trust. In Teamship, every member contributes uniquely, but they do so with a mindset of collaboration, understanding that the success of the whole is far greater than the sum of individual achievements.

In fostering Teamship, we create an environment where each person feels valued for their contribution and supported in their growth. It's a dynamic and fluid process where the roles of leader and follower often interchange based on the situation or need. True Teamship isn't about hierarchy, it's about synergy. It's about bringing out the best in each person and creating a space where ideas can be challenged, creativity can flourish, and everyone is invested in the success of the group.

Life is a journey of collaboration, of how we relate to other people and our companions in everything we do. Teamship helps us master our intentions because we can only go so far in life if we're on a journey alone. How we relate to others in every facet of life is how it all ties together. Teamship is how we create a fulfilling life with others.

The Power of Collaboration

Collaboration is the heart of Teamship. When we foster a culture of collaboration, we create an ecosystem where individuals feel free to share their thoughts, contribute their ideas, and solve problems collectively. Collaboration allows teams to achieve far more than they could on their own, bringing together diverse perspectives and skill sets to generate innovative solutions.

Teamship is about moving from "I" to "we" and shaping your team into a unit that thrives on collaboration, mutual respect, and shared goals. At the heart of Teamship is our ability to lead and nurture high-performing teams. In work and life, we can no longer rely on siloed expertise or individual excellence alone. Today's world demands collaboration, shared accountability, and collective innovation. A high-performing team doesn't just happen—it evolves.

In 1965, Bruce Tuckman introduced us to the *Five Stages of Team Development*,[53] a fundamental framework that still holds today, and it's through this lens that we can understand the evolution of Teamship. He identified the five stages of team evolution as: forming, storming, norming, performing, and adjourning. Let's take a look at each now.

---

[53] Lumen Learning. "Reading: The Five Stages of Team Development." *Principles of Management*. Accessed August 28, 2025. https://courses.lumenlearning.com/suny-principlesmanagement/chapter/reading-the-five-stages-of-team-development/#:~:text=Bruce%20Tuckman%2C%20an%20educational%20psychologist,norming%2C%20performing%2C%20and%20adjourning.

Stage 1: Team Forming — The Beginning of Teamship

In the forming stage, team members come together with excitement and anticipation but also with some degree of uncertainty. Participants ask, "Who is on this team?" and "What is my role?" Your role as a team leader isn't to dictate direction or force productivity. Instead, it's to foster relationships and to build trust. The greatest tool you have at this stage is *open dialogue*.

Use this exercise to help build team cohesion early on. Have team members pair up and ask each other, "Why are you here? What's your personal goal?"

While this may seem simplistic, it helps break down walls and create an environment where team members start to see each other not as colleagues, but as collaborators. After all, shared understanding forms the foundation of high-performing teams.

While writing this book, the cofounder of my current business exited the company to pursue another venture. While I anticipated this exit, it was a startling moment for the rest of the company. Caught by surprise, team members were feeling uneasy and uncertain about what this meant for the company and what the next chapter in our business would look like. For me, it was the perfect time to recalibrate, unite, and together form what the new team structure and vision of the business would be.

After three years in business, roles would be redefined and new opportunities for leadership would arise. In bringing my leadership team together, I helped frame the vision for exactly that. My goal was to help each member understand that while change possesses a level of uncertainty, it could also be tremendously exciting. We sat around a table and I asked everyone to look at the members there. In life, it's important to focus on who's here, not who isn't. It's important to focus on and build off of one another's strengths, not become bogged down in weaknesses. So, that's what we did.

I asked each leadership member to make a list of each person's strengths, both personal strengths and how they contributed to the team's success. We then went around and each person shared the perceived strengths of every other member of the team. The goal was to build commonality and reaffirm the strengths each leader at the table possessed. From there, we discussed why each person's strengths made them a valuable addition to the team. This allowed everyone to see that each of us fit together like a puzzle: every member of the team had an equally important contribution to the organization's success. After listening to the affirming words of each colleague, I challenged each member to define their current role as it exists today and how they feel this change in the structure creates an opportunity for them to enhance their role to take on more responsibility and create the pathway for personal development and professional growth.

A key takeaway from this exercise was that it's not only important how we see and perceive ourselves, but how the rest of the organization perceives and values our contributions. Leadership isn't merely a title, it's a set of qualities and standards. That's why it was important for each member individually, and collectively as a group, to identify the leadership standards we wanted to set for ourselves and others. How were we going to hold one another accountable? How were we going to hold ourselves accountable? In order to earn loyalty and respect, we must first embody those values and treat others with them. By coming up with a shared value and set of expectations, we were better able to understand one another's individual goals and get to the root of each person's "why."

Stage 2: Team Storming — Navigating Conflict with Courage

Once the team forming honeymoon phase ends, we enter the team storming stage. This is where differences of opinion, conflicts, and power struggles emerge. Many teams falter here, but I want to stress this: *conflict is not failure, it's growth*. It's the pressure that transforms team coal to team diamonds! As leaders, the key behavior we must nurture is the ability to embrace, manage, and resolve conflict constructively. This is where the heart of Teamship begins to form.

Teams in this stage must answer two critical questions: "How will we get this work done?" and "How will we work together?"

The goal isn't to eliminate conflict, but to *channel* it productively. Encourage open communication and create an environment where differences can be discussed respectfully. One powerful exercise here is discussing *team aspirations*. Ask: what are we striving for together? And, perhaps even more importantly, what are our *team values*? Spend time as a team to define those values, and you'll have a guiding light when times get tough. These practices are thoroughly explained in Practice 2 in Exercise 2.2: Aspirations, Values & Norms.

Stage 3: Team Norming — Becoming a Cohesive Unit

In the team norming stage, teams start to hit their stride. Team members begin to recognize and acknowledge each other's strengths, and team dynamics become smoother. This is also the stage where complacency can set in, and where you as a team leader must stay vigilant.

The key question now becomes, "How do we improve our efficiency and impact?"

The focus of the team dynamic should now shift from resolving differences to optimizing performance. The tools that really help here are *feedback* and *continuous improvement*. I highly recommend using the Situation-Behavior-Impact (SBI) feedback model to provide constructive feedback to team members. All team members should be introduced to this tool so they can use it and recognize when colleagues are using it. SBI provides a proven, structured feedback format for teams to continue refining their interactions and enhance their effectiveness.

It's important to remember that Teamship isn't just about harmony, it's about building momentum towards shared goals. Throughout this stage, leaders need to focus on ensuring all voices are heard and leveraging each team member's strengths.

In the prior stage we set the shared expectation that we would commit to receiving and delivering feedback. In this stage we're going to practice that by using the SBI feedback model (I'll outline it more in detail later on). The key components of this framework are to deliver feedback in real time, to be specific, and to focus on the behavior and impact it had on the team. By implementing this framework, each member of the team will almost immediately begin to feel empowered to address conflict and challenges head on, helping them become stronger in their individual roles and more cohesive as a team unit.

Stage 4: Team Performing — Achieving Excellence Together

When a team reaches the performing stage, something magical happens. This is where real Teamship lives. Teams operate with a shared sense of purpose, team dynamics are productive, and team focus is razor-sharp.

The key question now becomes, "What can we do to improve continuously?"

Google did an extensive study on what makes teams effective,[54] and they found five key contributing factors: *Psychological Safety*, *Dependability*, *Structure and Clarity*, *Meaning of Work*, and *Impact of Work*. A high-performing team excels in each of these areas. As a leader, it's your role to ensure that each of these factors is present. Let's break these down:

- **Psychological Safety:** Your team members need to feel safe to take risks and voice their opinions without fear of judgment. This doesn't mean there won't be disagreements, it means they feel secure enough to express them.
- **Dependability:** Can team members rely on each other to meet deadlines and fulfill their responsibilities? A culture of accountability and trust is nonnegotiable for high performance.
- **Structure and Clarity:** Everyone should be clear about their roles, responsibilities, and the team's goals. Without structure, teams can quickly fall into disarray.

---

[54] Google. "Understanding Team Effectiveness." *re:Work*. Accessed August 24, 2025. https://rework.withgoogle.com/en/guides/understanding-team-effectiveness?utm_source=chatgpt.com#identify-dynamics-of-effective-teams.

- **Meaning of the Work:** The work itself must resonate with team members on a deeper level. This is where purpose comes into play. People need to know that what they're doing matters—not just to the team, but to the world.
- **Impact of the Work:** High-performing teams believe that their efforts are making a difference, both internally and externally. Effective team leaders continually reinforce the broader impact of the team's work.

At this stage, the key question to ask your team is, "How are we doing as a team?" and then to allow space and grace to listen to their answers. An effective practice is to facilitate a feedback session where each person shares three strengths they feel they bring to the team and ask for constructive feedback from their peers. Teamship requires constant reflection, realignment, and improvement.

This is my favorite part of the framework because it's not only where the team starts to gel, but also when individuals start to recognize their growth, reaffirm their contribution, and where confidence starts to take center stage. This is where the team feels the most united and becomes the jumping off point for the next growth phase of the business. This is where expansion happens, margins increase, and when the team begins to embody a growth mindset where anything we put our heads together on becomes possible.

Stage 5: Team Adjourning — Celebrating, Recognizing and Reflecting

All great teams eventually disband. How you end a team's journey is just as important as how you begin it. The adjourning stage is where team members seek closure and reflect on their shared experience.

The key question is, "What do we take away from this experience?"

Effective leaders provide space for teams to celebrate their achievements and acknowledge the contributions of each member. A simple exercise for this stage is to hold a *team wrap-up meeting* where team members express gratitude to one another. Afterwards, encourage each team member to share one key takeaway that they'll apply to their next team experience.

In every leadership team and company meeting, we always start off with a gratitude practice, discussing what and who we're thankful for. By starting meetings with a gratitude mindset, we not only center and frame the conversations that follow, we also open ourselves up to better absorb takeaways. Recognizing one another's contributions, addressing challenging moments, and appreciating the assistance of others in collaborating to achieve shared success is crucial for team growth and development.

Key practices for recognition are detailed in the *Power of Gratitude* in Practice 10.

Feedback is a Teamship Super Skill

We create stories about people in our heads, especially when they disappoint us. This happens all the time. We see a behavior, assume we know why the other person acted a certain way, and then choose to react based on those assumptions. Within our companion sets, we have to start with the assumption that the people we interact with broadly intend to do the right thing. Sometimes, something gets scrambled or misinterpreted along the way, and the impact is far from what they intended. After all, if those people genuinely intended to harm us, why would we even be dealing with them?

There are many reasons to start with the assumption that our companions have positive intent for us. We assume that our family members wish us well and not harm, that our friends are our friends for reasons based on mutual emotional prosperity, that our work companions share the desire to accomplish our organization's goals and objectives, and that our life companions are with us because they want to show up and help us be our best selves.

The bonds of strong relationships strengthen when we have the tools and skills to navigate moments of unintentional hurt when they emerge. Being proactive in initiating a clarifying discussion will help navigate many interpersonal difficulties. After all, the only way to know what someone intended is to ask them, and the only way to let a person know their impact is to tell them. These essential conversations rarely happen, and for most people, they're hard to have. What results is that we're at risk of moving through our days in a tangle of misperceptions and actions based on incorrect assumptions, which doesn't bode well for strengthening the bonds of our relationships. So, what's the best way to initiate a productive feedback conversation to uncover why a person chose to behave a certain way that we believe resulted in a negative impact?

You can close the gap between intent and impact by clarifying the situation, describing the behavior, explaining the impact, and then exploring intentions. The proven SBI framework is considered the best practice for navigating conversations about these unexpected moments. That's because it's context-specific, focused on the behavior (and not the person), doesn't blame (but emphasizes impact on the receiver or group), and requests greater effectiveness (or impact).

Empower Others and Build on Their Strengths

Feedback skills aren't just for you as a leader. Empowering others with effective feedback skills too is a cornerstone of lasting leadership and successful Teamship, because it provides them with the tools and autonomy they need to take initiative and bring their best to the table. It's about trusting your team and encouraging them to take ownership of their work and working relationships.

Assume Positive Intent

Consider a scenario at work when a team member missed a deadline. Without realizing it, we might quickly label them as unmotivated or careless. This snap judgment can lead to frustration, resentment, and strained relationships within the team. But what if we start with a different assumption? What if we believe they generally intended to do the right thing, but something got lost in translation? Perhaps the instructions needed to be clarified, or unforeseen circumstances arose. By approaching the situation with this mindset, we open the door to a more constructive and empathetic dialogue.

In our daily interactions, it's easy to fall into the trap of making quick assumptions about others' actions and intentions.

This often happens subconsciously. Without even realizing it, we create narratives based on limited information. When someone disappoints us, fails to meet our expectations, or behaves in a way we find perplexing, we instinctively try to fill in the gaps with our own interpretations. Our past experiences, biases, and emotional states often influence these interpretations, leading us to conclusions that may not reflect reality. We often don't realize how much we project our own stories onto others, especially when they disappoint us. It's a natural human tendency—we observe behavior, make assumptions about the motives behind it, and then react based on those assumptions.

Provide Feedback Based on Positive Intent

By adopting a perspective of assuming positive *intent* within others, we shift from a mindset of judgment to one of curiosity and empathy. Instead of jumping to conclusions, we can engage in a constructive conversation to understand the underlying reasons for their behavior. This approach fosters a more supportive and trusting environment and paves the way for resolving issues more effectively.

With any companion, whether that be family, friends, colleagues, or life partners, starting with the belief that people generally have positive intent is crucial. Our family members, friends, and life partners typically wish us well, and our work companions share goals of achieving the organization's objectives. Trust is built on these respective foundations, so that assumption of positive intent is what will allow us to navigate moments of unintentional hurt or disappointment.

When misunderstandings do occur, having the tools and skills to address them can strengthen the bonds of our relationships. One of the most effective relationship practices at our disposal is giving and soliciting feedback with respect and care. But giving feedback can often be challenging, leading to discomfort for both the giver and receiver. Keep in mind that the objective of a robust feedback practice is to initiate clarifying conversations to foster understanding and growth. Feedback methods that focus too much on the person ("You did X.") rather than the specific behavior ("I observed Y.") often lead to defensiveness and communication breakdowns. Thankfully, there's a better way to have these conversations.

Exercise 8.1: The Situation-Behavior-Impact (SBI)™ Framework

The Center for Creative Leadership (CCL), a globally recognized organization focused on leadership development and research, designed the Situation-Behavior-Impact (SBI) framework[55] for navigating difficult feedback conversations. The SBI framework is a powerful tool that focuses on three key elements—Situation, Behavior, and Impact—to help provide feedback in a structured and constructive way. This approach is particularly effective because it helps clarify the situation, describe the behavior observed, and explain its impact—without blame. Many organizations have built on this original proprietary framework and modified it for various audiences. This version is the one I prefer as most applicable to the relationships in my life:

---

[55] "Use Situation-Behavior-Impact (SBI)™ to Understand Intent," Center for Creative Leadership, November 18, 2022, https://www.ccl.org/articles/leading-effectively-articles/closing-the-gap-between-intent-vs-impact-sbii/.

Step 1: Describe the Situation

Begin by clearly identifying the situation in which the behavior occurred. This step is crucial for setting the context and ensuring that both parties are on the same page. Your goal is to be specific and objective.

> **Example:** *"This morning at the 11:00 a.m. team meeting..." Pause.* Wait to continue until you know they have processed what you are bringing up.
>
> **Advice:** Be specific. Be succinct. Keep it objective and avoid interpretation.

Step 2: Describe the Behavior

Describe the behavior you observed. The key here is to be objective and avoid any interpretation or judgment. Don't talk about what you assume the other person was thinking or any motivation for the behavior. *Stick to what a third party would have seen or heard.* Anyone who observed what happened should agree with your behavior description. Don't get into your *interpretation* of the behavior or the *motives* or *intentions* you believe were behind the behavior. This adds subjectivity, making it easier for the other person to refute. Guide them away from *why* they did what they did—those are justifications.

> **Example:** *"You interrupted me while I was telling the team about the monthly budget,"* instead of *"You were rude."*

Advice: Clearly state the observable behavior, not whether it was justified. Don't say what you think *other* people observed. That adds *subjectivity*.

Step 3: Describe the Impact

Explain the impact of this behavior. How did it affect me, the team, or the project? Keep your observations factual.

Example: *"I was impressed when you addressed that issue without being asked"* or *"I felt frustrated when you interrupted our presenter because it broke his train of thought."*

Advice: Replaying in this way will likely make the person feel uncomfortable; let them. Your job is to be directly challenging and to show care at the same time. Avoid interpreting the impact *you think* this had on *other* people. Focus on the impact it had on you.

By mastering the art of giving and soliciting feedback with respect and care, you'll improve your team's effectiveness and contribute to a more positive and productive workplace culture. This skill is essential for any manager who aspires to lead with the empathy and effectiveness required to engage with others in all domains of life.

Further Your Feedback with Requests and Queries

Depending on the situation, you may choose to take the conversation further. This is where an R gets added to the framework expanding the SBI to SBIR—Situation, Behavior, Impact and Request. Here are two ways to extend the framework for two different desired outcomes.

The first, "*Requesting Changes to Future Behavior,*" is more common in work environments. The second, "*Explore Intentions to Deepen Understanding,*" is more common in less formal environments, such as relationships between companions.

Optional Step 4: Request Changes to Future Behavior

If appropriate, you can make a specific request for future behavior; this step is recommended for those in leadership positions. It could be as simple as asking the person to pause before interrupting in the future, or to be more mindful of their tone. It's essential to be clear and concise in your request. Consider going further and asking if they also have a request for you. Mutual requests evolve the feedback into a two-way conversation to foster mutual understanding and improvement.

Whether the other person does anything with your request is totally up to them. You've done your part in making the request. There's no need to convince them, and it's up to them regarding whether to heed the request. In other cases, you may rightfully expect the person to make the change. However, don't expect that one instance of SBIR will do the trick. You may need to use SBIR several times. After you've made the request, ask the person if they have a request for you. There are four responses they can give you:

1) Yes.
2) No.
3) Yes, with this modification.
4) I don't know—I'll get back to you tomorrow on that after I have a chance to think about it.

Optional Step 5: Explore Intentions to Deepen Understanding

A different and highly influential action is to inquire about the person's original intentions. This can reveal underlying motivations and open up a coaching style dialogue. Asking questions like, "What were you hoping to achieve with that?" allows for deeper reflection and understanding. Clarifying the gap between intent and impact builds trust and lays the groundwork for future growth. When you inquire about intention, motivation, or what's behind an action, you're essentially in a coaching conversation—one that can make a positive difference well before a performance review or disciplinary conversation. This is a key tool of a leader coach.

The Benefits of Effective Feedback

Incorporating the core SBI framework into your management toolkit will significantly enhance your ability to give and receive feedback. It reduces defensiveness, fosters open communication, and strengthens relationships within your team. More importantly, it cultivates a culture where feedback is seen not as criticism, but as an opportunity for continuous improvement.

Summary of Practice 8: Fostering Teamship

Your success won't be defined by your individual brilliance, but by your ability to inspire, lead, and empower others to greatness; that's why Teamship is the leadership skill of the future. High-performing teams evolve—they don't just happen. They require deliberate leadership, continuous reflection, and a commitment to collective success. Lead with Teamship, and you'll not just achieve goals—you'll exceed them; you'll not just build teams—you'll build legacies.

Teamship encourages collective ownership and shared responsibility. It promotes a culture where everyone contributes to the team's success, and where leadership is distributed, not concentrated. The future will demand leaders who aren't just great individual performers, but who can *build and lead* high-performing teams. Let's be clear—Teamship isn't a "soft" skill. It's the skill that will determine the success or failure of teams and organizations in the future. The workplace is changing rapidly, and the ability to foster high-performing teams will become the most valuable asset in any leader's toolkit.

Ultimately, fostering Teamship is about fueling a culture where individuals and teams can flourish. It's not about you as a leader—it's about what the team can accomplish together. By nurturing Teamship, you'll build stronger teams and inspire a future generation of leaders to continue the legacy you've begun.

Implications for Innerwork:

- Practice vulnerability to build deeper connections with others and reduce the negative impact of feeling isolated.

- Identify and embrace your quirks and uniqueness, fostering self-love while seeking personal validation and connection with others.
- Engage in self-reflection to understand your contributions, allowing you to bring your best self to every interaction and situation.
- Commit to long-term personal development, cultivating leadership and resilience within yourself for future challenges.

Implications for Teamship:

- Guide your team through the stages of development, from forming to performing, with practical strategies for fostering unity and collaboration.
- Create a space where team members feel comfortable sharing their ideas, discussing conflicts openly, and holding each other accountable.
- Lead with transparency and encourage trust-building activities.
- Continuously check in on the team's progress and dynamics to ensure alignment with the collective vision.

Practice 9

LEAD WITH AUTHENTICITY

You'll experience liberation when you finally begin living your most authentic life.

As I was sitting down to craft this practice, I went back and reread all of my notes in my iPhone, the place where I warehouse all of my innermost thoughts. It acts as a kind of journal, a stream of consciousness that includes my most intimate emotions, vulnerable feelings, fears, dreams, and aspirations—all tucked away in secret for my eyes only. I've made a habit of documenting whatever I'm thinking or feeling here, including thoughts I wanted to express but didn't know how, when, or with whom to share.

As I reviewed my notes dating back to 2017, there it was—the outline of the story of this book. Stored on my iPhone all this time and never ready to share—until now. Raw, unfiltered emotion I'd kept hidden from the world, dated and time-stamped. I relived the moments I was struggling with my confidence and all my action plans for how I intended to rebuild it, how I was terrified and didn't think I had the strength to keep fighting, and how I felt isolated in some relationships even though I was deeply loved by many companions in my life. There were also unanswered questions about how I would become a better version of myself, despite not knowing the path forward.

One of the notes I wrote to myself was titled "Chapter 1" of the book I hoped to write one day, dated November 28, 2020:

> It was 10:00 a.m. on the Monday before Thanksgiving. So many days—years, actually—had been a blur at that point in time, however, I remember that morning clearly. I was sitting around the conference room for my monthly team meeting with eight other colleagues waiting for my boss to arrive. Normally these meetings were cut-and-dry—we kept to business tasks—but today was different. Today my boss, a guy who never really gave people credit for much, came into the meeting and said in the spirit of Thanksgiving he wanted to go around the room and share why he was grateful for each member of the team. My hands clammed up and I got nervous about what he would say once he reached me. One by one he went through each member of the team, and then his eyes were on me.
>
> He said, "Bianca, you are the most optimistic and happy person I have ever met. You always have a smile on your face and you conduct every aspect of business with enthusiasm and

joy. You are no-nonsense. I ask Bianca to do something and her response is always 'on it' or 'done.' She follows up with me to confirm before I ever even need to follow up with her. Are you always just so happy? You would have no idea that she ever has a bad day in her life. No matter what's going on, she has a smile on her face and she comes into work ready to give it her all."

Truthfully, I think it would be a review that anyone would want their boss to say about them. It was certainly the nicest thing he had ever said to me, and I could tell everyone around the table was looking at me smiling. I knew in their head they were just as speechless as I was, but it was in that speechless moment that I couldn't help but think to myself, "What the fuck is wrong with me?"

While I'd been sitting around that table, laughing and smiling with my colleagues at 10:00 a.m., nobody, *nobody*, in the world knew that just a few hours earlier, I had peeled myself off of my father's couch after yet another sleepless night with an unrelenting emotional and physical hangover. Before I left and turned over "babysitting" duties to my uncle, I had to go into my grown father's room to make sure he was still breathing and that I could take a deep exhale that he had made it through one more night before I headed off to work for the day to be my happy, cheerful self. Not a single soul in the world knew that when I wasn't putting on my smile at work, I was tasked with sitting at my father's side to ensure he wouldn't kill himself. And that when the tears and pain became too much to bear, I became his late-night drinking partner to try to find some physical release from the god-awful nightmare we were both living every day.

As I sat around that table and heard those beautiful words, all I could think about was "If people only knew that I lost the will to live weeks ago. That I have no more fight in me. and all I want during this 10:00 a.m. meeting is to be three cocktails deep so I can already be on the trajectory of forgetting what the hell I'm going through. I don't think anyone would believe me. Would anyone get it? Did anyone feel the same way? Could anyone understand?" Maybe, but probably not.

My dad—my hero, my best friend, the strongest person I had ever known—was now a convicted felon, and that picture-perfect, happy-go-lucky life I thought I was living, well, that just wasn't in the cards for me anymore. The happy girl I had always been had become numb to life, numb to bad news, numb to relationships, and living on autopilot. There were so many days during that time period that were such a blur. I wish I could say it was days or even months,

MASTERING INTENTIONS

but it was years of exhaustion, of dread, of poisoning my body, and of destroying my relationships and not having a single regard for anyone but myself.

In this book, you may decide you hate me, you may love me, you may not be able to relate to a single thing I say, or you may bawl your eyes out because you feel like you're being heard for the first time ever. I'm not a therapist, I'm not an expert, I'm just a twentysomething year old woman who understands trauma, who has felt far too much pain, and, by some grace of God, is still walking this Earth. A girl who has manifested strength and positivity and who has survived, against all odds, and has become a better, stronger, wiser, and more loving person because of it.

This note hit a nerve. The moment I read it, I remembered exactly when I wrote it. But why had I put it aside? I spent so many years pretending everything was ok and putting on a strong face for the world. Forging forward with dominance, trying to survive. I so desperately wanted to open up to the world, but didn't feel safe to do so. I didn't feel safe to be my authentic self.

Until I did.

Until I realized that we all have stories, we all have tremendous pain, and we all have experienced heartache—as well as love, pure joy, and happiness. Our stories are what make us who we are: they shape us into the person we've become. The beautiful, strong, capable people that we are today. So why not own that? Why not become liberated by our stories, through connection, by way of becoming authentic and honest with ourselves and the world? That is strength. One of my favorite books is Brene Brown's *Daring Greatly*,[56] where she writes, "Yes, we are totally exposed when we are vulnerable. Yes, we are in the torture chamber that we call uncertainty. And, yes, we're taking a huge emotional risk when we allow ourselves to be vulnerable. But there's no equation where taking risks, braving uncertainty, and opening ourselves up to emotional exposure equals weakness."

This became the turning point for me; recognizing that vulnerability is not weakness, but the essence of connection. It's the most powerful, authentic force that bonds us with other human beings.

Find Your Voice and Tell Your Story

In business, as in life, your story is one of the most powerful tools you have. Your story sets you apart, resonates with others, and allows you to make authentic connections in everything you do. But how do you find your voice? How do you shape your personal narrative in a way that not only defines who you are, but allows others to see you as a unique individual with experiences and insights that matter?

I want to take you through a few key principles drawn from my own journey and the many incredible stories I've heard. I hope this will guide you on your own path to discovering and telling your own personal story.

---

[56] Brené Brown, *Daring Greatly: How the Courage to Be Vulnerable Transforms the Way We Live, Love, Parent, and Lead* (New York City: Avery Publishing, 2015).

Start With Authenticity: Your Story Begins with You

The first and most important step to finding your voice is realizing that your voice already exists. Too often, we look outward, thinking that we need to mimic someone else's style or replicate someone else's success to be heard. But the truth is, the most compelling stories always come from an authentic place within. Finding your voice is an essential step toward leading with authenticity. It's the process of peeling back the layers of societal conditioning, professional expectations, and self-imposed limitations to uncover who you are at your core. Your voice is more than just the way you communicate—it's the outward manifestation of your beliefs, experiences, and values.

To find your voice, you must first embrace self-awareness. This requires deep reflection on your experiences—both personal and professional—that have shaped who you are today. It involves asking yourself difficult questions that you have already thought about in previous practices, such as:

- What are the key moments in my life that have defined me?
- What core values drive my actions and decisions?
- What strengths do I bring to the table, and what weaknesses do I need to acknowledge?
- What do I stand for, and how does that translate into my leadership?

Once you've gained clarity around these aspects, it's time to tell your story. Storytelling is a powerful leadership tool, and when done authentically, it has the potential to build deep connections.

Authenticity means accepting that your experiences, struggles, and successes are all valuable. Stop filtering out the messy parts of your life. The most powerful stories are often born in those messy parts. In speaking with others while writing this book, I quickly realized that real storytelling comes from actual experiences. Your story is your unique narrative, and the best way to tell your story is to start with where you are. Own your journey—whether it's the challenges you've faced, the failures you've experienced, or the triumphs you've celebrated. All of it matters because it's uniquely yours.

In professional settings, we learn valuable tools to navigate the business world, but our greatest asset is still who we are and how we've gotten here. When you share your story authentically, you give others permission to be vulnerable as well. You create a safe space where they feel comfortable sharing their own experiences, which fosters trust and deepens relationships. Your voice becomes a beacon that others can rally around, because it's grounded in truth and integrity.

Embrace the Power of Vulnerability

As I've reinforced throughout this book, sharing your story requires vulnerability. We live in a world that often celebrates perfection and success, but the truth is vulnerability is what connects us—it's what makes your story human. In exploring my own vulnerability and putting it on these pages, I sought to create something that resonated with others. In your own journey, don't shy away from the parts of your story that make you feel vulnerable, scared, or nervous—the parts that make you feel like you're standing in a room naked and exposed. It might be the fear of failure, the anxiety of taking risks, or the uncertainty of your future—whatever it is, lean into it. That's because when you're willing to share the struggles, people relate better. Vulnerability is the bridge that allows others to see themselves in your story. This is especially crucial in leadership, where you need to inspire people to take action.

Understand the Structure of Your Story

In any great story, structure is key. Whether you're writing, giving a business presentation, or sharing your personal narrative, how you structure your story matters. But here's the thing: while structure is important, it doesn't have to be rigid. You don't need to follow a formula or paint by numbers. Instead, think of your story as having a beginning, middle, and end. The beginning is where you introduce the listener to who you are, where you've been, and what has shaped you. The middle is where the challenges and conflicts emerge—the obstacles that have tested you, pushed you, and forced you to grow. And finally, the end is where you reflect on how those challenges have shaped the person you are today.

Your story, like my own, is still being written. We're always in the middle of our respective stories—we're living and creating them every single day—so don't feel pressured to have everything figured out. It's okay to acknowledge that you're still in the process of becoming; that's what makes your story dynamic and relatable.

Be the Protagonist, But Include Others

Think of yourself as the protagonist of your own story. What are the driving forces in your life? What are the obstacles you've faced? By framing your experiences as part of an evolving narrative, you give yourself and your audience a sense of purpose and direction. While your personal story is yours, it's also about the people who have shaped your journey. Think about the companion characters in your life—your mentors, family, friends, and colleagues. Each of these people plays a role in your story. Some will be sources of inspiration, others will serve as obstacles or antagonists. But all of them contribute to the richness of your narrative.

One of the most valuable things you can do as you tell your story is to acknowledge the people who have helped and shaped you along the way. This not only shows humility, but also highlights the interconnectedness of our lives. In business, as in storytelling, no one is an island. Success is built on relationships and the connections you make with others. The final practice in this book is about gratitude, and by utilizing the practices of gratitude you can build on the way you shape and share your story.

As you reflect on your own journey, think about the lessons you've learned from the people around you. What have your relationships taught you about yourself? How have others helped you grow or challenged you to be better? These are the elements that add depth to your story and make it more than just a list of accomplishments.

It's About Resolution, Not Perfection

One of the biggest mistakes I'm told that people make when telling their story is thinking that they need to have a perfect ending. I'm sure we can all agree that life isn't perfect. So if we're being honest and vulnerable with ourselves, how could our story be? Don't try to tie your story up with a neat little bow. In storytelling, the ending is where the emotional resolution happens, or how it's ongoing. It's about evolution, the journey, and progress. It's where the audience feels the impact of everything that has come before. In your own story, think about what lessons you've learned, what insights you've gained, and how those experiences have shaped the person you are today.

Storytelling is an art. Authentic storytelling is about more than recounting facts or experiences: it's about sharing the emotions and intentions behind those experiences and presenting your truth in a way that resonates with others and invites them into your journey. Authenticity in storytelling is rooted in the principle of congruence: that what you say, feel, and do are in alignment. This is critical in leadership because people can sense when a story is fabricated or embellished; they can tell when a leader is trying too hard to present an image rather than sharing an honest truth.

On the other hand, when your words and actions align, people trust you more. They see you as credible and are likely to buy into your vision. Authentic storytelling isn't about manipulation or crafting the perfect narrative, it's about sharing your experiences with humility and sincerity, allowing others to see the person behind the title. Your career, your personal life, and your relationships are all part of a continuous story that is still unfolding—and that's the beauty of it. You don't have to have all the answers right now. Your story is still being written. Ultimately, what matters is not that you've reached some ultimate success, but that you've learned to navigate the challenges along the way.

Keep Expanding Your Toolbox

Seeing as your story is ever evolving, telling it is like building a toolbox: each experience, each lesson, and each person you encounter adds a new tool to your collection. Over time, you learn how to use those tools to craft your story more and more effectively. For me, every project I've worked on has added something new to my toolbox. I've learned different techniques and keep refining them. In the same way, your personal and professional experiences will keep expanding your abilities. Don't be afraid to learn from others, seek advice, and borrow techniques from people you admire. Talk to your mentors and your peers—every conversation is an opportunity to pick up a new tool and a new way of thinking about shaping your impact.

Take Ownership of Your Narrative

No one else can tell your story for you. It's yours to shape, share, and own. In business, as in life, there will always be people who will try to define you or tell you what your story should be. But the only person who can truly tell your story is you. Take ownership of your narrative; don't let others define your path or dictate your voice. Your experiences, your values, and your vision are uniquely yours. Use them to create a story that reflects who you are and what you stand for.

When you tell your story, whether in a job interview or in casual conversation, tell it with confidence. The world needs to hear your voice. Let me say that again: *the world needs to hear your voice.* Stories change lives. They are the heart and soul of inspiration, connection, and impact. Your story has the power to inspire, connect, and create change, but it all starts with finding your voice and owning your journey. The world is ready to listen.

Define Your Brand Through Storytelling

Your brand is how the world perceives you, and storytelling is one of the most effective ways to define that brand. A leader's brand isn't just about what they do; it's about why they do it. It's about the values they stand for, the vision they hold, and the impact they seek to make.

Through storytelling, you can define your brand by sharing the "why" behind your actions. What drives you to lead? What experiences shaped your leadership style? What impact do you want to have on your team, your industry, and the world?

To define your brand through storytelling, start by identifying the key themes of your journey:

- What are the core values that have guided you throughout your career?
- What challenges have you faced, and how have they shaped your perspective?
- What legacy do you want to leave behind?

Exercise 9.1: Telling Your Story

In this book you've already completed exercises that help you find your purpose and build your Journey Map (Chapter 1). Those exercises will also help establish the emotional awareness and set the foundation for this exercise: a three-act structure to tell your personal story:

- **Act 1 — The Beginning:** Reflect on where your journey started. What was your environment? What beliefs or values were important to you in your early life? Who and what were your early influences?
- **Act 2 — The Conflict/Challenges:** Identify the moments where you faced obstacles or turning points. What decisions or actions did you take in response to these challenges? How did these moments change your perspective?
- **Act 3 — The Resolution/Insights:** Consider how those experiences have shaped who you are today. What insights have you gained? How are you different now compared to when you started this journey? Where do you see yourself going next?

Take the key moments and themes from your Journey Map and write a short, one-page version of your three-act personal story. Focus on clarity and authenticity; don't worry about making it perfect, this is just a starting point. The goal is to begin articulating your voice and story in a way that feels true to who you are.

By answering these questions, you craft a narrative defining your brand. Your story becomes a reflection of your authentic self, and through storytelling, you can communicate that authenticity to others. Your brand isn't just a professional identity—it's an extension of your personal values and experiences.

To set the stage for how to start your story telling, let me start by sharing mine.

Growing up in a close-knit Italian family, family values of loyalty and respect were ingrained in me at a young age. I was the eldest daughter of two incredibly hardworking, entrepreneurial, and resilient parents.

My mother has led a life of unwavering commitment to her values; I watched her time and time again make the hard decisions because they were morally right—she never took the easy route that compromised her beliefs. Fiercely independent, she raised us to know our worth, be honest, and live with compassion. Through her actions, she taught me sacrifice: sacrificing short-term gains for the long-term reward in order to build an authentic life filled with love, even when life challenges us. An aspirational career woman and an equally remarkable mother, she paved her way through a male-dominated industry yet made sure she cooked dinner for us every night so we could eat as a family and spend time around the table talking about our day.

My father was a visionary businessman. Growing up with nothing, he had something to prove—to himself, to his family, to his friends, and to the world. He worked tirelessly to build an empire and taught me how to be a fighter: that even when the chips are stacked against you, if you put your head down, show up every day, and keep working hard, eventually it will pay off.

Living through my parents' divorce challenged a lot of the important values I was raised with. All of a sudden, I was put between the two most important people in my life. With loyalty and honesty embedded in me, who was I to be loyal to now? How could I embody honesty when I realized being honest was hurting the people I loved most? I was raised to be strong but experienced tremendous internal conflict. This manifested by developing a very strong and positive exterior while internally I felt isolated and deeply misunderstood. Thankfully, cognitive behavioral therapy helped me overcome years of struggling with depression and helped me develop an astounding level of self-awareness. I realized I have an incredible ability to manage—and remain positive—during times of uncertainty. In fact, a part of me seeks chaos because it's when I'm challenged the most to be creative and problem solve.

I learned that life changes quickly and that we have to be the makers of our own happiness; we can never allow other people to determine our self-worth or value. I recognized the power of independence and taking risks, and learned that perspective changes through experience. I also learned to live with compassion and empathy because, while it was easy for me to hide what was going on inside, we never really know what someone else is experiencing behind closed doors. I also realized that running away, traveling the world and looking for answers, will change awareness and exposure, but it won't fix what exists within us. The only way to work on your happiness and face your demons is through intense vulnerability and a commitment to work on yourself.

These resounding lessons took me through the most challenging years of my life: unexpectedly losing a close friend in my early twenties, and then two more the year that followed; being in a car accident that left me with chronic pain issues; the seven years of being on the front lines with my father as he filed for bankruptcy, lost his business, was incarcerated, and then managed to rebuild thereafter; the long-term relationship that ended; the countless business opportunities and partnerships that didn't pan out as expected; and the countless highs and lows through my professional journey.

I'm the beautiful sum of each of these experiences and of every single one of these people. I'm the creator of my journey. Life doesn't happen to me, but *for* me, and the only commitment I must make is to myself: to become better, to become stronger, to learn continuously, to work fiercely, and to give and receive love to those I cherish most. This is my brand. This is the heart and soul of my business: to live authentically through every chapter of my life, to share with others the possibility of doing the same, to create hope where it may not currently exist, and to pay it forward. Because the same way I'm a sum of every experience and person, I hope one day I can be part of someone else's equation. With goal setting, vision, and direction, I'll move on the path of life. There's no right or wrong path, just the one I'm on, and it's up to me to make the journey along that path the most rewarding possible.

Own Your Brand

Once you've defined your brand, the next step is owning it. Owning your brand means standing firmly in your identity and values, even when external pressures try to push you in different directions. It's about being confident in who you are and what you stand for. In order to wholeheartedly own your brand, you must be consistent, responsible, and committed.

Consistency is key to building trust. When people see that your words and actions are aligned over time, they develop confidence in your leadership. They know what to expect from you, and that predictability fosters loyalty.

You must also be willing to take full responsibility. This means being accountable for your actions, decisions, and the impact you have on others. It's about understanding that your brand isn't just how you present yourself, but how others experience you. Develop an unwavering commitment to your values. There will be moments when you're challenged to compromise your beliefs or take an easier route. In these moments, staying true to your brand—your authentic self—is crucial. When you own your brand, you lead with integrity, knowing that your actions are a reflection of your deepest principles.

Refine Your Brand

Like your story, as you grow both personally and professionally, it's natural that your brand will evolve too. Change is inevitable, both in life and leadership. Over time your priorities, goals, and even values may shift. Redefining yourself as this evolution happens is a necessary part of personal and professional development, but it's essential to do so while remaining authentic. Refining your brand ensures that it stays relevant, impactful, and aligned with your evolving self.

Refinement starts with reflection. To redefine yourself authentically, start by acknowledging the changes you're experiencing. What new values have emerged in your life? How have your goals shifted? What lessons have you learned that are shaping your future direction? Periodically assess how your brand is being perceived by others and whether it still aligns with your current goals and values. Solicit feedback from trusted colleagues, mentors, and clients. Ask them how they perceive your leadership and what areas they believe you can improve in.

Redefining yourself doesn't mean abandoning your past. It means integrating new insights into your existing framework to improve how you communicate your story. As you gain new experiences, your story will naturally evolve. Incorporate these new insights into your narrative to keep it fresh and relevant. Share your continued growth with your audience, showing them that you're committed to lifelong learning and improvement.

Ultimately, the key to refining your brand is to remain authentic while adapting to change. It's about staying rooted in your core values while allowing your leadership style to evolve with new knowledge and experiences.

Integrity in Leadership

At the heart of authentic leadership lies integrity. Integrity is the foundation upon which trust, respect, and credibility are built. It's the practice of aligning your actions with your values, even when no one is watching. Without integrity, authenticity becomes hollow—because authenticity without a moral compass is merely self-expression, not leadership.

In leadership, integrity manifests in the consistency of your actions. It means that you do what you say you'll do, and you follow through on your promises. It means making decisions that align with your values, even when those decisions are difficult or unpopular. Integrity requires courage, because it often means standing firm in your beliefs in the face of opposition.

Leaders with integrity build cultures of trust. When your team knows that you act with integrity, they're more likely to follow you, support your decisions, and work collaboratively toward shared goals. Integrity fosters loyalty, because people know that they can rely on you to act with fairness, honesty, and respect.

In the end, leading with authenticity and integrity is about more than just achieving success—it's about leaving a lasting impact. Authentic leaders and storytellers inspire others not only to follow them, but to embrace their own authenticity. They create a ripple effect of honesty, trust, and connection that extends far beyond their immediate sphere of influence.

By leading with integrity and authenticity, you set the example for others to do the same. You show that it's possible to be both successful and true to yourself, and in doing so, you create a legacy that endures.

Summary of Practice 9: Leading with Authenticity

Vulnerability and living authentically aren't just important in personal relationships, but essential tools in leadership and business. Storytelling is the root of connection, but in order to understand, tell, and share your story, you must embrace vulnerability and remain authentic. Vulnerability is a strength—it bridges gaps and allows others to relate to you on a much deeper, human level.

Each of our stories are complex, so embrace that complexity. The magic of your brand is in the complexity of your story. By living authentically and leading with vulnerability, you'll build trust, inspire others, and ultimately find liberation in becoming your true self.

Implications for Innerwork

- Step into your authentic self by embracing vulnerability and sharing your personal story.
- Reflect on your values, strengths, and areas for growth, and lead from a place of integrity.
- Remember that authentic leadership requires being transparent about your intentions and creating meaningful connections through storytelling.
- Build self-awareness to understand how your actions impact those around you and consistently strive to lead with compassion and purpose.

- Lead with integrity, ensuring your decisions reflect your values, even in difficult situations.

Implications for Teamship

- Foster an environment where team members feel safe to be authentic and share their stories.
- Encourage team members to define their own personal brands and align them with the team's goals.
- Lead by example with integrity, ensuring your actions consistently align with your words.
- Use storytelling as a tool to build deeper connections and inspire your team to lead with purpose and integrity.
- Use authenticity to build a strong team culture based on trust, vulnerability, and shared values.

Practice 10

UNLOCK THE POWER OF GRATITUDE

Gratitude shifts perspective—and everything in life is about perspective.

Café Gratitude, a plant-based restaurant chain, is known for encouraging customers to engage in practices of affirmation and gratitude as part of their dining experience. Upon entering, a "Question of the Day" prominently posted invites customers to reflect on positive aspects of their lives and discuss the question with their dining companions. That simple act of prompting customers, "What are you grateful for today?" transforms the typical dining experience into a moment of reflection and personal growth. Cafe Gratitudé incorporates creeds directly into its menu design, too.[57] Every menu item carries an affirmation that helps guests reflect on positive emotions and cultivate an attitude of gratitude. For example, dishes have

---

[57] "Menu," Café Gratitude, accessed December 1, 2024, https://cafegratitude.com/pages/cafe-gratitude-menus.

names like "I Am Magical," "I Am Grateful," "I Am Fabulous," and so on.

As we order, we vocalize these affirmations, creating a direct connection between what we consume and the positive traits or feelings we're affirming in ourselves. This process is designed to promote mindfulness, encouraging patrons to not only think about what we're eating, but also to reflect on our inner state and emotions as we enjoy our meal. The very act of ordering food becomes an exercise in self-affirmation. By stating phrases like "I Am Thriving" or "I Am Peaceful," we engage in a form of positive self-talk. This reinforces the café's mission to encourage personal growth and intentional living through a simple, yet powerful practice, while allowing us patrons to affirm our aspirations or current state of being while cultivating a sense of gratitude for the nourishment we're receiving.

The Power of Gratitude

It's taken me decades to feel grateful for my hardships: grateful that I struggled with depression as a young child, because now I'm strong enough to fight to be alive; grateful for my parents' divorce, because it allowed me to become independent and strong; grateful that my father was arrested, because now I'm wise enough to know how quickly life can change; grateful to have experienced tremendous loss, because it forced me to realize how fragile life is; grateful to have had failed investments and appreciate that money doesn't dictate happiness; and grateful to have had failed business partnerships, because now I know what it takes to build successful ones.

Practicing gratitude becomes a beacon of hope and transformation. After all, life is too short to focus on what's missing or what went wrong. Embracing gratitude isn't merely a passive acknowledgment of what's good in life, it's an active choice that can profoundly shift our perspective, foster mental health growth, and catalyze personal development.

Gratitude is far more than a respectful "thank you"—it's a powerful mindset that can shape our daily experiences, relationships, and overall well-being. It bridges appreciation and mindfulness, encouraging us to be present and acknowledge the abundance in our lives, no matter how small. In a world that often pushes us toward constant achievement and consumption, a regular practice of gratitude invites us to pause, reflect, and focus on what truly matters.

Whether through mindful choices in what we consume or intentional acts of kindness within our communities, gratitude becomes a way of life. It's a practice that influences how we view ourselves, our relationships, and the world around us. Businesses like Café Gratitude embody this mindset by creating spaces where gratitude is an integral part of the dining experience, helping people to practice appreciation in their everyday interactions. They remind us that gratitude is a momentary emotion and also a way to engage with life more fully and intentionally.

When was the last time you truly felt grateful for something? Why did you feel grateful, and how did you express it? Did your gratitude ripple out to affect other areas of your life?

Exercise 10.1: Gratitude Letter

Gratitude has the power to make life happier and more fulfilling. When we feel grateful, we get to relive the positive memories from our past. And when we express gratitude to others, it strengthens our relationship with them. However, a quick or casual "thank you" can often feel empty, lacking the depth that true gratitude deserves. In this exercise, you'll have the chance to experience what it's like to express heartfelt gratitude deliberately and thoughtfully, inspired by psychologist Martin Seligman in his book *Flourish: A Visionary New Understanding of Happiness and Well-being*[58]. Here's how to apply it:

Step 1

Close your eyes and think of someone still alive—someone who, years ago, said or did something that positively changed your life. This is a person you never truly thanked in a meaningful way, but someone you could meet face-to-face in the near future. Do you have someone in mind?

Step 2

Write a letter of gratitude to this person. Aim for around three hundred words, and be specific: explain precisely what they did for you and how it impacted your life. Describe the emotions and thoughts that arise for you when you think about these experiences and why it has stayed with you. Share what you're doing now, and let them know how their actions continue to influence you. Make it meaningful! Close by reiterating your gratitude and expressing your hopes for continued connection or mutual support.

---

[58] Martin Seligman, *Flourish: A Visionary New Understanding of Happiness and Well-being* (New York City: Free Press, 2011).

Step 3

Reflect. After writing your letter, take a moment to reflect on how the process felt. Did it bring up any emotions? Did it help you see your life or relationships in a new light? Write down these reflections in your notebook. Consider integrating this gratitude practice into your daily or weekly routine. This might involve writing more letters, keeping a gratitude journal, or simply taking a few moments each day to acknowledge the good in your life. Think about the companions who have supported and inspired you, and don't keep your appreciation to yourself! Tell the people around you how much they mean to you.

Step 4

Call the person and arrange a visit—but don't reveal the reason for the meeting. The surprise adds a special touch to the experience. When you see them, take your time and read the letter aloud.

Meaningful Gratitude Goes Beyond Good Manners

Studies have shown that practicing gratitude can lead to a host of benefits, from improving mental health to enhancing relationships. Engaging regularly in brief activities designed to cultivate a sense of gratefulness (known as a gratitude intervention), has been shown to be one of the most effective positive psychological interventions.[59]

A meaningful gratitude practice is about recognizing the positive in our lives—whether it's someone's kindness, the opportunities we have, or even small moments of beauty amidst difficulty. Gratitude doesn't erase the challenges we face, but it allows us to find value and meaning in both the good and the hard times.

At its core, gratitude is a conscious, positive emotion we feel when we recognize and appreciate something—whether it's tangible or intangible. From a young age, we're taught to express thanks for gifts or kind gestures. But gratitude goes beyond social niceties: it's about consciously appreciating the everyday moments, the small joys, and the things that often go unnoticed. True gratitude requires more than just saying "thank you" out of habit, it requires us to genuinely feel and acknowledge the positive impact of what we're thankful for.

Gratitude is an accessible tool we all have, capable of improving not just our own well-being, but also the lives of those around us. It has the power to shift our perspective, transforming what we have into something more. Gratitude turns scarcity into abundance, denial into acceptance, and chaos into order. It provides clarity in confusion, helps us make sense of our past, and brings peace to the present while inspiring hope for the future.

---

[59] Yu Komase, Kazuhiro Watanabe, Daisuke Hori, Kyosuke Nozawa, Yui Hidaka, Mako Iida Kotaro Imamura, and Norito Kawakami, "Effects of gratitude intervention on mental health and well-being among workers: A systematic review, "*Journal of Occupational Health* 63, no. 1 (January/December 2021), https://doi.org/10.1002/1348-9585.12290.

Use Gratitude to Shift Your Focus

Instead of dwelling on what we lack or what isn't going right, gratitude allows us to focus on what we have and what's going well. This shift in perspective fosters greater resilience, better mental health, and deeper connections with others. Gratitude helps us reframe our challenges, appreciate the present, and approach life with a sense of abundance and joy. In essence, gratitude is a simple yet powerful practice that can transform our outlook on life and, ultimately, lead to a greater sense of happiness and fulfillment.

A regular practice of gratitude has been shown to bring numerous benefits, both mentally and emotionally. Research in the field of psychology, particularly positive psychology, highlights gratitude as one of the most impactful practices for enhancing well-being. Studies show that people who consciously take time to count their blessings are not only happier, but also less prone to depression. But how does it work?

Exercise 10.2: What Went Well

Dr. Seligman also recommends a complementary practice known as the "What Went Well Exercise." His research team at the Positive Psychology Center and the University of Pennsylvania discovered that people often spend too much time focusing on the negative aspects of life, which can lead to anxiety and depression.[60] By shifting our focus to what is going well and cultivating gratitude instead, we can counteract these negative tendencies.

---

[60] YouTube. "What Went Well Exercise." *YouTube*. Accessed September 9, 2025. https://www.youtube.com/watch?v=EMGwU7zNo-U&t=55s.

Step 1

Each night for the next week, take ten minutes before going to bed to reflect on your day. Write down three things that went well today and why they went well. You can use a journal or your computer, but the key is to have a written record. These three things don't have to be life-changing events; small, everyday moments work just as well. For example, you might write, "I had a great conversation with my friend today," or "I finished a project at work that I had been putting off."

Step 2

Next to each positive event, answer the question: "Why did this happen?" If you wrote about a great conversation with your friend, you might explain it happened because "I made time to reach out" or "We both had a free moment to connect." If you noted the completion of a project, your answer might be, "I was focused today and managed my time well" or "My colleague helped me finalize the last details."

Reflecting on why positive things happen may feel strange at first, but stick with it for a week. Over time, it becomes easier and more rewarding. Pushing past the skepticism ingrained by cultural conditioning and our Brain Bully, Seligman assures that we will feel "happier, and possibly even hooked on this exercise."[61]

At its core, gratitude is about shifting focus from what is lacking to what is present and positive. This shift in perspective is transformative. When we embrace gratitude, we reframe our

---

[61] Martin Seligman, *Flourish: A Visionary New Understanding of Happiness and Well-being* (New York: Free Press, 2011), chapter 2.

experiences and circumstances, altering how we perceive the world around us.

- **Focusing on Positives:** Instead of dwelling on what we don't have or what's going wrong, gratitude encourages us to recognize and appreciate the abundance already present in our lives. This shift fosters a sense of contentment and optimism, even in the face of adversity.
- **Reframing Challenges:** Gratitude helps reframe challenges as opportunities for growth rather than insurmountable obstacles. By acknowledging the lessons and silver linings in difficult situations, we can approach problems with a more balanced and resilient mindset.
- **Cultivating an Abundance Mindset:** Adopting a gratitude practice helps cultivate an abundance mindset, where we see life's opportunities as plentiful rather than scarce. This perspective not only enhances our overall outlook, but also increases our motivation and enthusiasm for pursuing our goals.

It's important to remember that gratitude is a mindset and feelings of gratitude are internal. Gratitude is a way of seeing the world from a perspective of *what's abundant*. It's about pausing to appreciate the people, experiences, and good in our lives. Think of experiencing a mindful moment in your day, to pause and reflect on what you're grateful for. It could be during your morning coffee, on your commute, or before you go to bed. It's like taking a moment to watch a sunset; the sunset doesn't change the challenges you faced during your day, but that feeling of peace and appreciation you allow yourself for the good that's around you is much like the feeling of gratitude.

Gratitude is also linked to better sleep, lower stress levels, and stronger immune systems. But beyond the physical benefits, gratitude helps cultivate a positive outlook on life. It's like a muscle—the more you use it, the stronger it becomes. When you acknowledge the good things in your life, you start to notice more of them. Gratitude changes your perception, making you more attuned to the positives around you. It's like learning a new name and suddenly starting to hear it everywhere.

The impact of gratitude on mental health is profound and multifaceted. Research and clinical observations consistently highlight how gratitude contributes to emotional well-being and mental health growth:

- **Reducing Stress and Anxiety:** Regularly practicing gratitude has been shown to reduce stress and anxiety levels. By focusing on positive aspects of life, we can diminish the impact of negative thoughts and worries, leading to a calmer and more centered state of mind.
- **Enhancing Emotional Resilience:** Gratitude fosters emotional resilience by reinforcing positive emotions and helping us navigate life's ups and downs with greater ease. It encourages a positive outlook, which can buffer against the impact of stress and adversity.
- **Improving Sleep and Physical Health:** Gratitude has been linked to better sleep quality and overall physical health. By promoting relaxation and reducing stress, gratitude contributes to improved sleep patterns and a stronger immune system.
- **Building a Positive Self-Image:** A gratitude practice enhances self-esteem by shifting focus from perceived deficiencies to acknowledging strengths and

accomplishments. This positive reinforcement builds confidence and a healthier self-image.

Embracing gratitude isn't just about enhancing mental health; it's also a powerful tool for personal growth and development. It paves the way for deeper self-discovery and facilitates meaningful progress in various aspects of life:

- **Encouraging Self-Reflection:** Gratitude invites us to reflect on our experiences, values, and relationships. This self-reflection fosters greater self-awareness and understanding, guiding us toward personal goals and aspirations.
- **Strengthening Relationships:** Expressing gratitude towards others strengthens social bonds and fosters deeper connections. It enhances empathy and understanding, which is crucial for building and maintaining healthy relationships.
- **Inspiring Personal Development:** The practice of gratitude inspires a growth mindset, where we see challenges as opportunities for learning and improvement. By acknowledging and appreciating our progress, we're motivated to continue pursuing our personal and professional goals.
- **Creating a Sense of Purpose:** Gratitude helps us recognize the impact of our actions and the significance of our relationships. This awareness fosters a sense of purpose and fulfillment, driving us to contribute positively to our communities and make a meaningful difference.

Gratitude might seem like a simple concept, something we were taught as kids, but it's not just a childhood lesson; these are profound practices that can change how we experience life, relationships, and careers. Incorporating gratitude into daily life requires intentionality and consistency. The intentional practice of gratitude and recognition will enrich your life in ways you might not even imagine.

Building a Culture of Gratitude

Imagine a world where gratitude and recognition are the norms, not the exceptions. It's a place where people feel valued and appreciated, kindness is reciprocated, and positive energy flows freely. By practicing these principles, we can create that kind of environment in our own lives.

There's something special about receiving gratitude or recognition from someone you respect or look up to. It's like when a professor, boss, or parent compliments your work—it just feels different. In a work environment, for example, people value recognition from their managers more than from their peers. Top-down recognition can be a game changer. It can open doors, boost morale, and even propel careers forward. But this idea isn't limited to the workplace—it's relevant in all areas of life. When you acknowledge the efforts of someone who looks up to you or when you recognize the kindness of someone you admire, you're creating a ripple effect of positivity and motivation.

Let's bring this closer to home and talk about gratitude in our relationships. For most people, we put tremendous value on our relationships, whether with friends, family, or colleagues. Gratitude has this incredible ability to deepen our connections with others. When we express gratitude to someone, we're not just saying "thanks," we're telling them that they matter and that their actions have meaning to us.

This simple act of acknowledging what others bring into our lives can transform our relationships. It strengthens bonds, fosters trust, and creates a space where love and kindness can thrive. And it's not just about the big moments; it's about the little things, too. Gratitude makes the ordinary extraordinary, turning everyday interactions into meaningful exchanges.

Shifting your mind and attitude to recognize and convey gratitude in all experiences is a practice. Thankfully, through documentation and reflection, you can exercise this brain muscle to become routine in your habits. which will have a ripple effect in your relationships.

Documenting Gratitude

I'm always of the mindset that taking silent time to reflect and write is when the most intentional and honest thoughts come to mind. I encourage you to take a few minutes each day to write down three things you're grateful for. It could be anything—a kind word from a friend, a beautiful sunset, or even just a moment of peace. This exercise aims to empower you to develop a consistent gratitude practice that will enhance your self-awareness and self-management skills. By focusing on the daily positive aspects of your life and the people who contribute to them, you'll build a stronger, more resilient mindset. Remember, gratitude is more than just a polite "thank you"—it's a powerful tool that can transform your outlook on life, improve your well-being, and enhance your relationships.

Exercise 10.3: "I'm Grateful"

In the spirit of the positive affirmations of Café Gratitude, think about the moments that have brought you joy and the challenges that have helped you grow. This exercise is meant to be introspective and reflective, so create an environment that allows you to focus fully.

Step 1

Ground yourself by sitting comfortably and closing your eyes. Take a few deep breaths, inhaling slowly through your nose and exhaling through your mouth. With each breath, allow your body to relax and your mind to settle. Let go of any distractions or worries and bring your attention to the present moment.

Step 2

Reflect on the people, experiences, and aspects of your life that you're grateful for. For this exercise, your Reflection Prompt is: "I am grateful for…"

Step 3

Write down anything that comes to mind, big or small. This could include personal achievements, acts of kindness, supportive friends or family, opportunities that have come your way, or simply the beauty of nature around you. Think about the moments that have brought you joy, the challenges that have helped you grow, and the individuals who have supported and inspired you.

Step 4

When thinking about challenges, hardships, or losses, reflect on the gains you've had in relation to them. What have you learned about yourself? How did it shape you? How did it force you to grow in a way you may not have without the experience?

Gratitude is Powerful

The gratitude exercises that I practice are simple yet profound. They have the ability to bring more joy, fulfillment, and connection into our everyday experiences. But it starts with us. Gratitude and recognition are like seeds; when you plant them in your daily life, they grow into something beautiful. By making gratitude and recognition a habit, we can influence the people around us to do the same. It might be as simple as writing a thank-you note, acknowledging someone's efforts, or just telling someone how much they mean to you. These small acts can have a huge impact.

Summary of Practice 10: Unlocking the Power of Gratitude

If there's one theme that should be carried throughout this book, it's that life is a journey of constant growth and evolution. Mental perseverance and fortitude are necessary to embrace the lessons life is teaching us. Fostering strong mental health is essential to experiencing growth in life, and embracing a practice of gratitude is the healing power behind improving one's mental health.

By committing to these practices, we improve our own well-being while making the world around us a little brighter. And the best part? It's contagious. When we start to live with a grateful heart and an open mind, others will too. We create a cycle of positivity that lifts everyone up.

Implications for Innerwork

1) Embrace gratitude for positive experiences and hardships, using challenges as opportunities for growth and self-reflection.
2) Regularly pause to reflect on the good in your life, both large and small, to foster a sense of appreciation and mental well-being.
3) Use gratitude as a tool for self-awareness, recognizing how far you've come and how much you have to offer.
4) Document your gratitude to reinforce a positive mindset, strengthen self-awareness, and track personal growth.
5) View life's challenges as opportunities to learn, grow, and become stronger, and let gratitude guide your reflections on how these experiences shape you.

Implications for Teamship

1) Foster a culture of gratitude within your team by regularly recognizing and appreciating each member's contributions.
2) Encourage team members to acknowledge and appreciate each other's efforts.

3) Encourage team members to reframe challenges as opportunities for collective growth, using gratitude to maintain a positive and balanced perspective.
4) Incorporate regular team exercises, such as writing gratitude letters or sharing reflections, to build a strong foundation of appreciation and recognition within the group.

What's Next? Let's Be Intentional Together

It's my hope that as you finish this book, your biggest takeaway is that you're the creator of your own life. The purpose of this book is to empower you to take control of where you want to go next by recognizing that when you commit to shifting your mindset, anything is possible by living with intention.

> *You are resilient. You are strong. You are in control. You are merely a fraction of the person that you are meant to become.*

As you close these final pages, I hope the questions you start asking yourself are: What now? What do I do with these ten principles? Where do I start?

You probably already know that it won't be easy and that personal development and growth don't happen overnight—it compounds over time. So, when you close this book, give me a year. Commit to me for a year; better yet, *commit to yourself for a year*. I promise if you start putting in the work today, one year from now you'll be unrecognizable. In just one year, your entire life will change. By implementing the disciplines and practices I've shared with you in this book, I've transformed myself into a lifelong learner with a winner's mindset and have been able to reinvent myself time and time again.

This book contains countless exercises, frameworks, and practices for you to follow, and I now want to leave you with your final practice, a way to tie it all together: The daily practices that you can put to work the moment you read the final words of this chapter.

Start Today

The moment you close this book, I want you to start with the two most immediate practices: *positive self-talk* and your *gratitude practice*. Commit every single morning to these practices. Your day begins here—with positivity and gratitude. Promise yourself for thirty days you'll start every single morning with these practices. Then a month from now, go for another thirty. Sixty days from now, your outlook of the world will be different, your opinion of yourself will be stronger, and your appreciation for others will be enhanced. You'll learn to become your own hype person and your own biggest advocate and cheerleader. You'll problem solve with confidence and handle conflict with ease. Your new mindset will start to dictate all of the success and outcomes that will follow.

Ninety Day Roadmap

Remember, these practices are building blocks, each one stacking onto the next. While still tremendously beneficial individually, you'll maximize their impact when you start to incorporate each of them in sequence.

Month One

In your first thirty days I want you to focus on the world around you—the people, places, and events—bringing your past into the present. The next thirty days are all about setting the foundation for your self-awareness journey.

In the first week, start building your *Life Journey Map*. I hope this book has given you the opportunity to reflect on your biggest life moments—both the highs and lows. Now, it's time to map them out. Start to embrace vulnerability and really dive deep into the life sequences that have gotten you to where you are today.

In week two, start to focus on the people who have and who continue to shape your life. Let's build out your *Companion Audit*. Who's currently participating in and cocreating your life? What relationships are working well and which are no longer serving you? It's time to start manifesting intentional relationships.

In week three, you now have the elements needed to *write your story*. You've spent the two weeks prior mapping your life events and identifying the people who play the biggest role in your life, now it's time to take ownership of your narrative. Think about your three acts and write your first draft. Remember, your story is ever evolving and constantly changing; this is just the start.

In week four, end the month with a *gratitude letter*. This is the bow that will wrap the past three weeks together. How do you find gratitude for the people in your life, the events they've been a part of, and how they've shaped your narrative? Put it down on paper, share it with them if you're ready, or hold onto it for a bit longer if you aren't quite there yet.

Month Two

In month two, we dive deeper into the Innerwork. How do we use what we learned about ourselves the prior month and build on that for the future? This is where we start activating intentions and manifesting.

In the first week, build out your *Strengths Spotlight*. I'm hoping the past thirty days have left you feeling stronger and more empowered, so now it's time to become even more confident and motivated. When we work from a place of strength, we're better able to overcome challenges and fuel resilience to optimize performance.

In week two, let's *activate your intentions*. What three qualities do you need to focus on right now in order to become the person you wish to be? What feelings do you wish to embody? What three qualities or values do you want to begin wholeheartedly embodying? How are you going to do this? Pick your three intentions, commit yourself to them, and remind yourself of them every day.

By week three, it's time to start *manifesting*. With clarity, your strengths, and a refined focus on your intentions, how do you turn intentions into reality? Through active manifestation. Be specific about what you want to achieve, visualize it clearly, and take consistent steps toward it. Remember that manifesting your future isn't passive—it's an active process that requires dedication and belief in yourself. Are you going to begin journaling? Will you create a vision board? Are you practicing daily visualization tactics? Are your actions in alignment? What are you going to do today to begin acting as if you've already achieved what you want?

With continued focus on the future, in week four, let's *futurecast*. You have already begun manifesting, but how can you actively begin planning for major life events you know are likely to occur in the next five years? Identify them. If these major life events were to happen, would that impact your actions today? Would they alter the decisions you make? Would you change how you spend your time and/or money?

Month Three

Your first sixty days revolved around looking inward and outward. In many ways they should have helped you better understand your journey and the people who are playing a part in it—the people and events who dictate your purpose and power. In the next thirty days, let's focus on creating lasting impact.

In week one, start by examining your *habits*. Are your habits in alignment with your manifestations? Do they align with your values? Are they keeping you on track with your intentions? Are you prioritizing your compansionships? Think about your routines and disciplines. Are you maintaining consistency? Are you holding yourself accountable? If you haven't been consistent with your self-talk and gratitude practices, why not? If you have, how do you feel today? What new habits do you want to begin incorporating into your life? How are you going to do so?

In week two, let's do a financial audit. Through the *Financial Mapping* exercise, begin to look at your relationship with money. Where and how are you currently spending your money? Are your spending patterns moving you towards or away from your goals? Are your saving habits in alignment with your intentions?

In weeks three and four, utilize the *Mastery Journal* to check back on your progress. Remember the Mastery Journal is episodic and routine; it's intended to assess your progress and see if you're staying in alignment. Have you done what you said you were going to do? Do you feel proud? How have these exercises added value? Have you grown as a person because of them? Are you interacting with your companions better?

Ninety Day Lookback

By now you're ninety days in. Remember that I promised you that you can change your life in a year? Well, the first fourth of it is set up for you. Hopefully by now you'll have incorporated daily, weekly, and monthly practices and done each of them multiple times. Now it's time to reflect on how you're feeling.

Over the past ninety days, did you recognize your growth? What has *made you proud*? Refer back to the What Made You Proud framework and focus on what you've done since the first time you closed this book. Has your perspective changed? Has your self-awareness improved? Have you grown as a companion?

You now should have done enough reflection on your journey and progress that you're able to recognize trends, habits, and behaviors, and have a new commitment to your values. Now it's time to write your *purpose statement*.

I am _____ (name) and my purpose is to _____ (insert action) so that _____ (insert desired impacts).

Write it down and leave it next to your bed. Put it on a sticky note and attach it to your computer. Make it your home screen on your phone. Whatever you decide to do it with, make sure you look at it every single day.

Every ninety days from now, I want you to spend thirty minutes with your personal statement. Put it in your calendar—a thirty-minute time block—every ninety days. Each time you come back to this, I want you to ask yourself: are my actions aligned with my purpose? Are my actions achieving the desired impacts? Do I still feel connected to my purpose statement?

Six Month Check In

The further it gets from the day you put down this book, the easier it will become to veer from these principals. But remember, accountability and consistency are instrumental to creating lasting impact. At this point in time, continue to reflect on the work you've put in and how far you've come. Go back and review your *personal story*. Does it still feel authentic? Revisit your *Mastery Journal questions*. Are they still guiding you? Revisit your *gratitude letter*. How did it feel writing and sharing this letter? Is it time to write one to someone else?

After you've completed the exercises personally, how are you able to bring them to your teams? How can you use them to enhance Teamship? Begin to incorporate the *SBI framework* and the *Five Stages of Team Development*. Have you been able to foster a *culture of gratitude*? Are you practicing positive *self-talk for teams*?

One Year From Today

Pick up your phone and mark one year from today in your calendar—that's right, when I promised you that your life would look different. I'm even going to take it a step further because we're in this together. Email me through www.BiancaDAlessio.com. Add me to your calendar invite on the anniversary date for when you finished this book and started *mastering intentions*.

One year from today, I want you to look back on all of it and ask yourself:

- How has positive self-talk changed the way you view yourself?
- How has gratitude impacted your relationships?
- What have you manifested that has become reality?
- How have you activated intentions around the three words you committed yourself to over the past year?
- How has future casting impacted how you spend your time and decision making?

Mastering intentions isn't a one-time task, it's a lifelong journey. Don't wait for the perfect moment, the right opportunity, or a future version of yourself to emerge. You have the tools, the knowledge, and the inner strength to begin living with intention *today*. Each small step brings you closer to the empowered, purpose-driven life you're meant to lead.

Visit my website at www.BiancaDAlessio.com to continue the journey and for exclusive access to workshops, courses, events, executive coaching, and more.

Embrace the power of mastering intentions and build the life and legacy that you envision for yourself—you have everything you need.

Let's be intentional together!

Acknowledgments

No great endeavor is accomplished alone, and this book is no exception. *Mastering Intentions* is the result of countless lessons, challenges, and triumphs—and I am beyond grateful for the extraordinary people who have shaped my path, lifted me higher, and reminded me why resilience and intention matter.

To my mom—you are the strongest and most inspirational woman in my life. Every day, you have been a role model, not just to me but to everyone around you. You have proven that no barrier is too high, no glass ceiling unbreakable. Through your relentless drive, grace, and unwavering belief that women can achieve anything, you have set the standard for how I show up in the world. Your ambition and integrity have shaped the woman I am today, and I hope to always embody that same tenacity and serve as a role model the way you have done for me.

To my dad—you are resilience personified. Life has tested you, challenged you, and thrown obstacles in your path, yet you have never stayed down. Your ability to rise, again and again, has given me the foundation to do the same. You have shown me that setbacks are never the end of the story—only an invitation to come back stronger. Your perseverance and unwavering belief in me have been my greatest sources of strength, and I carry that lesson in everything I do.

To my siblings—you are my best friends, my lifelong partners in adventure, and my greatest reminder that family is everything. I feel so lucky that we have been able to experience every life chapter together, growing side by side in ways most people only dream of. I am endlessly proud of the people you are becoming and grateful to walk through life with you.

To my grandparents—you have shown me that the best things in life are not easy, but they are always worth fighting for. Your love and unwavering dedication—not just to each other but to our entire family—are not only a testament to partnership, but to the power of devotion, sacrifice, and commitment. Your relationships have taught me that true love isn't just about the easy moments, but about showing up, through the challenges, the triumphs, and the everyday in between.

To my love, Dwight—our souls were bound long before we met, and finding you has been the most beautiful affirmation that what we seek with intention, we attract. You are my greatest manifestation—proof that love arrives exactly when and how it's meant to. From the moment our paths crossed, I knew you weren't just part of my story, but the place my heart had always been searching for. Thank you for being my partner in every sense—for standing beside me, for challenging me, for dreaming with me, and for loving me in a way that is deep, pure, and unshakable. True connection isn't found, it's created, and with you, I have found the love and partnership I always knew existed but never imagined could be mine.

To my friends—to have lived our memories from childhood to adulthood together is a gift that many people go their whole lives never knowing. That we have stayed by each other's sides through every chapter is a true testament to the strength of our bond. The years we have shared, the memories we have created, and the unwavering support we have for one another are irreplaceable. I am endlessly grateful for the friendship, love, and loyalty that have remained unshaken through the years.

To The Masters Division—this book is not just a reflection of my journey, but of the collective force that stands beside me every day. Your hard work, commitment, and trust allow me to push boundaries, lead with purpose, and build something greater than myself. I am endlessly grateful for your dedication and the energy you bring to our shared vision.

To my clients—thank you for entrusting me with your dreams and vision. Thank you for allowing me to be a part of your story—it is a privilege I never take for granted.

To my mentors—thank you for your wisdom, your challenges, and your belief in my potential. You have pushed me beyond my limits, reminded me that no setback is ever final, and equipped me with the tools to navigate the highs and lows of both business and life.

To Babson College—where my entrepreneurial mindset was sharpened, my confidence was built, and my ambition was fueled.

To Sigma Kappa—an incredible sisterhood that has shown me the power of strong women supporting one another. The values of friendship, loyalty, service, and personal growth became a guiding force in my life, shaping how I lead with heart and remain values-driven.

To CliffCo—thank you for both mentorship and friendship, for your belief in me, and for the opportunities that have helped me step into my full potential. Your guidance has been a pivotal force in my journey.

To the *Selling The Hamptons* team—the cast, production crew, and network—sharing the screen with such talented, driven individuals was an honor, and I'm grateful for the camaraderie, passion, and energy we brought to every moment.

To all my former employers, coworkers I have worked alongside, and those who have shaped my career—thank you for believing in me, recognizing my potential, and providing opportunities that pushed me forward. To those who challenged me to be better, pushed me beyond my limits, and expected more from me than I sometimes expected from myself—I am forever grateful.

To the friends and fellow wanderlusts I've met on my travels—thank you for the lessons, conversations, and perspectives that have shaped me. Every place, culture, and story has left an imprint on my soul, broadening my vision and deepening my appreciation for the world.

To my readers—this book is for you. Your hunger for growth, your determination to rise above adversity, and your commitment to mastering intention inspire me daily. If even one page of this book empowers you to take control of your story and step into your full potential, then every hour spent writing it was worth it.

And finally, to every obstacle, every "no," and every moment of doubt—I see you, and I thank you. Without you, I wouldn't have found the strength to push forward, to build, to rise.

Here's to the journey ahead—may we all live with intention, embrace the challenges, and build the lives we were meant to lead.

About the Author

Bianca D'Alessio is the star of HBO Max's acclaimed series *Selling The Hamptons*. Recognized as the top real estate broker in both New York City and state, Bianca founded and directs one of the top real estate brokerage teams in the United States, and she manages a $10 billion international real estate portfolio.

Having rebuilt her career through adversity, Bianca attributes her success to the art of mastering intention. She emphasizes the vital synergy between personal branding and business culture, advocating for the transformative power of manifestation, mindset control, and resilience in achieving exceptional success across all facets of life.

Bianca now shares her journey and insights in *Mastering Intentions: 10 Practices to Amplify Your Power and Lead with Lasting Impact*, where she delves into practical strategies and life-changing principles that empower individuals to unlock their full potential and thrive in today's competitive landscape.

Bianca is an alumna of Babson College. She is regularly featured on *Forbes*, *Fox*, *Medium*, *The New York Times*, *Inman*, and *The Real Deal*. She is often interviewed by Fox Business News, CNN, Bloomberg, Mansion Global, and *Forbes*, and she has a weekly real estate column in *Money Magazine*.